The SCHOOL BOARD FIELDBOOK

Leading With Vision

Mark Van Clay

Perry Soldwedel

A Joint Publication

Solution Tree

AMERICAN ASSOCIATION
OF SCHOOL ADMINISTRATORS

555 North Morton Street
Bloomington, IN 47404

800.733.6786 (toll free) / 812.336.7700
FAX: 812.336.7790

email: info@solution-tree.com
www.solution-tree.com

Printed in the United States of America

12   11   2   3   4   5

FSC
Mixed Sources
Product group from well-managed
forests and other controlled sources
Cert no. SW-COC-002283
www.fsc.org
© 1996 Forest Stewardship Council

ISBN 978-1-934009-44-4

Acknowledgments

This book is dedicated to all of the past, present, and future members of boards of education, members who give so unselfishly of their time and talents that public education can truly and successfully be a universal system of learning for all.

In addition, we are grateful for the opportunity to learn from districts who are members of the Consortium for Educational Change. The mission of the Consortium, a network of Illinois school districts and professional organizations, is to improve student achievement by assisting member districts and schools to become collaborative, high-performing organizations. The Consortium is where the authors first met and where they have collaborated ever since. Many of the references in this book come from the work of partners who help the Consortium do its work.

Visit **go.solution-tree.com/schoolboards** to download the reproducibles in this book.

Table of Contents

About the Authors

Mark Van Clay has accepted U.S. Department of Education Blue Ribbon School recognition as both principal and superintendent, each in a different school district. He is also a regular contributor to the Consortium for Educational Change, an Illinois-based network that focuses upon continuous organizational improvement. He has written and presented on a variety of educational topics, including the use of educational data, the school district scorecard, a shared-revenue collective bargaining model, and teacher training in instructional organization and motivation areas. He has worked with over 100 board members in three school districts and has been defining and refining his thinking on strategic, tactical, and operational roles.

Perry Soldwedel is the director of continuous improvement for the Consortium for Educational Change, a nonprofit consortium of 65 school districts—mostly in the Chicago area—that work together to accelerate behaviors and actions leading to improvement. He serves as a coach and consultant to school district leaders as they strive to improve their performance results. He also leads external review teams at both the district and school levels to provide organizations with feedback related to continuous improvement frameworks. His expertise includes shared leadership, strategic planning, collection and measurement of data (and its analysis), customer service, and alignment of standards, assessments, and instruction.

In the past, Perry was a district superintendent, assistant superintendent for curriculum and instruction, technology director, principal, assistant principal, and elementary and middle school teacher. He has taught continuing education classes for the University of Illinois.

Preface

What compelled two superintendents with more than 30 years' experience between them to write a book about the role of a school board?

Actually, there are four good reasons. First, the roles of the board and the superintendent often intersect, sometimes smoothly and sometimes painfully. Yet a partnership between board members and superintendents (or their leadership equivalents) is absolutely essential if a school organization is going to move forward. This partnership need not be serendipitous or dependent upon personalities or moods. From our experiences, we know that there are specific role attributes and habits that one can adopt to become a successful partner. We want to share those attributes and habits so that both board members and school leaders can intentionally incorporate them into their own behaviors.

Second, it seems to us that the school board role in common practice is often more complicated and frustrating than it really needs to be. Given that board members are citizens who generally join a board for the best of reasons, we hope that if we could describe the board role in clear words, with practical examples, board members might feel more of the joys than the frustrations of board membership.

Third, good board members are essential to effective and innovative school systems. If this book can help make more board members effective in their role, then more school systems will become the effective, innovative systems that are required to meet the educational needs of the 21st century. We see a direct link between successful board members, successful educational organizations, and successful students who will be prepared for the challenges of an increasingly complex, multicultural, and technological world. And we don't just want board members to be good—we want them to be *very good*, to meet the "gold standard," because that is what society wants of today's schools.

Fourth, faced with the challenges of achieving high expectations for all children, we know how important it is that school board members understand how to use data to make good decisions. A high-performing school district must build a data system that identifies, tracks, monitors, analyzes, and responds to key performance indicators of success. It's critical that this system extend from the boardroom to the classroom. If this book can clarify the board's role in monitoring performance results and can provide insight in how other stakeholders can align their work to drive those results, then more school systems will demonstrate accountability to the public.

Board membership can be exciting, energizing, and enormously fulfilling. But much of what it takes to reach the gold standard of board membership doesn't align with what most people initially bring to the board table. In this book, we'll explain why this is so and what can be done to practice board leadership at its highest, most effective levels, by applying principles, tools, and strategies that come from best-practice research on successful boards in education, healthcare, and business.

Achieving the gold standard certainly is challenging; it involves a learning curve for each board member. But the rewards of meeting the challenges are well worth it. The roadmap we offer will help shorten the learning curve and make learning the lessons much faster and easier.

1

The Learning Curve: What Makes Serving on a School Board Unique?

As a new board member, you may be told that there's always a "learning curve" before board service becomes familiar and intuitive. That's true. In fact, your previous experiences probably don't translate easily into your new role because board service is so different, and often counterintuitive.

Consider, for example, the fact that a board member cannot simply call or email the rest of the board and "work things out." In most states, open-meeting laws dictate when and how board members can communicate with each other. These laws ensure that the work of the schools is as public as possible. But by so doing, public laws restrict boards in ways that don't make your work any easier.

You may have decided to become a board member because you had an idealistic wish to serve the community. After all, you're taking on a job that will demand a lot of your time and energy, for no material gain whatsoever. Yet you'll confront very difficult decisions that often won't be clear to the public, and you'll seldom, if ever, be complimented for your hard work and selfless service. In fact, just the opposite: You'll likely hear from at least a few angry parents and disgruntled neighbors before your board tour is up!

You also may have joined the board with specific ideas about what needs to be done in the school organization to "make things work as they should." After all, how hard can it be? Virtually everyone went to school (most to public school), and there are public schools everywhere, most of which have been here for a long time. So, you can surely do this, right?

Yes, you can—but not without first going through a learning curve. This chapter will explain why your previous experience, no matter how successful, won't fully prepare you for board service. We'll also explore why your past and present professional successes, as well as your intelligence, common sense, and intuition, aren't enough to figure out how to become a good board member. Once you understand how unique your new role is, you'll start to see how becoming an effective board member can be well within your grasp.

What makes serving on a school board so complex? It shouldn't be. Schools are part of the local community, and you're well grounded in what your community is like. You come to the board with a set of skills that have proven successful in your own profession; applying them to a school setting should be simple and should guarantee success. You're also giving back to your community by serving on a school board. People will praise you for your dedication to public service, right?

Not so fast. In fact, serving on a school board is one of the most challenging tasks you'll encounter. But there are specific things you can do to meet those challenges and make your service one of the most rewarding experiences that you'll ever have.

Your experience offers some potential advantages to your board role. But just as you wouldn't be able to translate your present experiences to a different cultural and language setting without adapting to that environment, so you'll have to make translations of your own to the very different culture called public education. You and the other board members never will complete the tasks before you because the more you accomplish, the more you will learn about different tasks that need to be accomplished. Nonetheless, hopefully you will conclude your time on the board with satisfaction and the feeling that you've made a real difference for children. Figure 1-1 illustrates the important issues that make board service unique and complicated. With time, you'll learn how to accommodate them all.

Figure 1-1: Challenges for School Board Members

Managing the Volume of Information

As a board member, you'll receive a great deal of information, and managing it can be daunting. Copious materials for board meetings alone—packets brimming with agenda and action items, meeting minutes, background reading, data presentations, administrative recommendations, correspondences, hard copies of PowerPoint, and other types of presentations—will demand a personal organization and filing system.

Because meeting topics tend to recycle, you'll find it worthwhile to organize records of past actions and to be able to access that information easily. However, you should know that the administration can do much of this for you, using electronic tools, and thus your storage commitments should diminish over time as you become more comfortable with the administration archiving historic records on your behalf.

In addition, you will receive committee packets on specific topics, in electronic and hardcopy form, which will require your attention and, occasionally, an immediate response. There will be frequent correspondence between you and the superintendent or board president to raise questions or clarify or expand upon previous writings. You'll receive and need to respond to seemingly endless emails, from both the administration and the public. Finally, you may well feel that the administration is sending you countless articles and other writings as background information on topics to be considered at board meetings. This volume of reading material might seem overwhelming, and you may be tempted to skim it or skip it altogether.

Although you'll have to develop your own selective approach to this information flow, remember that from the administration's perspective, each piece of information is important. Administrators send you materials to read because they are trying to ensure that all board members receive the same information; written materials are the main vehicle by which the administration guarantees that you become fully informed in a timely fashion. Of course, actually managing to do all this reading is a discipline that you'll have to develop on your own.

Assuming Responsibility for All Children

Board service confronts you with this question: Who will you represent, your child or all children? In theory, the answer is obvious, but in practice it can be far more difficult. For example, what if your child is an eighth grader and you know as a parent that his or her math program needs to be upgraded? Are you willing to let the process of study and research take place for a year—as it should—to account for the needs of the board, administration, and teachers? Or will you attempt to rush the process so that your child doesn't miss out on the new program? Another example: If your neighbor's child has been suspended from school, will you fight this action simply because of your relationship with your neighbor and so disregard what may have occurred that caused the suspension? Or will you support the suspension because the principal correctly followed board policy and thereby risk frosty relations with your neighbor?

By assuming a board role, you become responsible for *all* children and for policies, rules, and procedures that guarantee that each student is treated fairly. In short, you become the guardian of the rights of all, not just a few.

Being Constantly "On Call"

When you first become a board member, you'll probably be shocked that other people, including your friends and neighbors, treat you as one "24/7." You probably conceived of your new role as a part-time, unpaid commitment to community service that comes third in your priorities, after your family and your profession. You'll soon find, however, that community members view you as a board member first, and their perspective will prevail over yours.

This means that you'll be fair game for questions and opinions about the school organization, the teacher, or your neighbor's child; about when after-school sports, concerts, and activities are scheduled; and about many other decisions, regardless of whether they were made by the entire board, the superintendent, or other administrative staff. You'll be a board member at neighborhood picnics, your place of worship, the supermarket, parent-teacher conferences, and everywhere else you go in the community.

Your board role will be assigned to you by your constituents on their terms and according to their schedules, not yours. You won't be able to remove your board hat, no matter how intent you may be in putting board issues aside for the moment. In short, you've permanently, if unknowingly, given up your "civilian" life to serve on a board.

When constituents can't contact you, your spouse may become a board member by proxy, which is rarely a role that spouses are willing to graciously assume. The best thing a spouse can say, from the very beginning, is, "I'm not on the board and am not involved in any of the board decisions or deliberations. You'll have to talk to my husband [wife]." Saying words like these may be exasperating at first, but will eventually result in the desired effect.

These issues arise for new board members in particular, because constituents look upon you as a fresh channel for community influence. Your inexperience makes you a magnet for constituent questions and opinions, often because community members also may view you as more accessible and subject to influence than those "jaded" individuals who have been on the board longer and have put up shields against the public. And right now, you probably don't *want* to shield yourself from the public.

In fact, you haven't yet learned the details behind complex board decisions that look simple to the public. Once you understand those intricacies, you'll probably become more focused on the complexities of the issues your board faces, and less so on the constituent interpretations of those issues. The more experienced you become, the fewer the constituent complaints and lobbying tactics you'll encounter.

Understanding the Business Paradigm

No one thinks of a public school system as a "business." Yet it's a very complex business—one that is heavily statutorily regulated, usually unionized, responsible for large employment costs, policy-laden, and financially challenged. At the same time, we expect schools to be models of fiscal and programmatic efficiency—to "do more with less."

Facing Public Education Realities

And yet, a school system *isn't* a typical business by any means and can't be run like one. School organizations don't have profit margins, and no one receives stock options;

it's impossible for a school district to declare bankruptcy. Schools don't produce a final "product," for their success in educating children isn't judged until those children are contributing members of society, long after they're out of school. And although the school system has no quality control over its "raw materials"—children—it's expected to produce predictable educational results according to prescribed standards. Its employees are largely guaranteed employment for life (through the tenure system), which the average citizen doesn't favor. Very few non-educators have a true and accurate appreciation regarding how difficult successful teaching really is, and laypeople are increasingly critical of educators and schools even when objective data regarding overall performance are positive. A school system's real "board of directors" is not a board at all, but the taxpaying public. Schools can't make money; they have to ask for it from taxpayers. In most states, school boards also must conduct their business in the public eye, unlike corporate boards, business owners, and stockholders, who seldom are accountable to the public for their decisions.

Responding to Political Reforms and Mandates

Many of the "reform" efforts that impact the work of public schools are driven not by educators, but by politicians, who typically have little understanding of school's inner workings. Not all reforms have negative effects, but most do not build on the good work schools are already doing or align with research on best practice in education. Many educators feel this is the case with No Child Left Behind (NCLB). NCLB has the right intent—that all public school systems in America help each child reach his or her educational potential—but its regulatory prescriptions and interventions often run counter to that intent. Yet left on their own, public schools usually don't willingly or comfortably embrace change. In trying to move a school organization forward, a board must find a balance between the forces of politically driven reform efforts and an inherent resistance to change.

Applying Systems Thinking

Public school institutions are slow to change and have deep cultural walls that must be scaled before real change can occur. This calls for a systems-thinking approach grounded in the belief that an institution is complex and naturally resistant to change, unless change is thoughtfully and carefully planned and executed (as a strategic plan, for example). Even a board's best ideas won't become operational realities unless their planning and implementation reflect the cultural and structural realities of the organization. Successful change happens *within* school organizations, not *to* them.

Often, a school district is a system of schools rather than a school system (see chapter 2), meaning that its key structures and processes are unaligned between different sites in the district. A challenge for board members is to hold all stakeholders—staff, students, parents, and the other community members in the decision-making process—accountable for the common things that everyone needs to do well.

Building Successful Partnerships

Public schools don't operate in vacuums. Because they're tax-supported, public schools are expected to serve the community beyond the children who are their immediate responsibilities. In many places, public schools are the center of community activities and social interactions, and have policies that allow for public access on a regular basis. Yet this openness to serving the community might sometimes run counter to the public's expectations of organizational efficiency. So boards must strike a balance between being open and being efficient—a balance that the community feels is fair and sensible.

School boards, when successful, are the ultimate example of the idea of partnership. While the board as a whole has immense authority, no individual member can make anything happen. This compels successful boards to develop sophisticated partnership behaviors to move the organization forward. Collaboration and mutual trust among board members, administrative staff, and teacher association leaders aren't just desirable; they're essential.

Meeting Stakeholder Needs

A school board doesn't operate in a vacuum; it's ultimately accountable to the community that placed its members in office, by either election or appointment. Its ultimate measure of approval comes at times of referendums or board elections. No matter what actions a board takes, the community it represents is continually judging those actions.

Accordingly, the board must foster collaborative partnerships with unions, parent-teacher organizations, and management. Local stakeholders include parents, children, staff (teachers, support personnel, and administrators), neighboring school systems, businesses, and real-estate brokers. Regional, state, and national stakeholders such as politicians, nonlocal businesses, institutions of higher education, and policymakers at all levels of government are also interested in what the board does. The board is answerable to all of them, either directly or indirectly.

All groups in the school organization need to "pull the rope" in the same direction to move the organization forward. For although a school board has impressive authority, its ties to numerous stakeholders greatly reduce its exercise of that authority. A school board is *representative* and must always act from that perspective to succeed.

Supporting Internal Accountability

The school board is ultimately responsible for defining the degree of accountability *within* the organization by setting and monitoring key indicators of success. Those indicators should reflect performance over time (trend data) and provide opportunity to compare progress against other schools (benchmark data). The board must cede its direct evaluation of accountability to the superintendent, as we shall see in chapter 2. Boards set direction for internal evaluation, but don't carry it out or monitor it—a task left to administrators and staff—unless they're operating outside of their prescribed role.

Defining Mission, Vision, and Values

These terms describe the fundamental beliefs that are held by the organization and defined in a strategic plan. The board promulgates these beliefs through its statements and actions. Individual boards can alter such core values to some extent, but since these beliefs are aligned to the community's own mission, vision, and values, they're meant to endure many changes in board and other school leadership. Mission, vision, and values are the bedrock upon which the board conceives and articulates change.

For example, the belief that "all children should achieve to their full potential" dictates certain commitments that the school organization makes to all children, regardless of their ability or talent. In turn, these commitments affect decisions about financial allocations, staffing, programming, resource allocation, and professional development. These decisions would be very different if the core belief were "All children will reach a common prescribed level of measurable achievement." Under this belief, the organization's commitment to children would "cap" how much a child is expected to learn, and resources and personnel would be allocated differently as a result.

If the school organization already has its distinctive mission, vision, and values, then a board must either embrace them and make its decisions accordingly or seek widespread community support to challenge them. If the school organization doesn't have clearly defined mission, vision, and values, then the board must collaborate with others within and outside of the organization to identify them—preferably through a comprehensive strategic planning process. As the board makes decisions and considers future options, it must adhere to the school organization's core beliefs; implementation of board decisions will fail if the values of the board conflict with those of the community it serves. To align board and community missions, visions, and values is no small task, but alignment will set the school district's culture for years to come.

Setting Goals and Priorities

Goals and priorities identify how the school organization will express its core beliefs. While they don't articulate exactly what to do, goals and priorities do describe big-picture targets that the organization hopes to meet within a prescribed amount of time, typically 1 to 5 years; they also usually include some measurable standards for success. For example, from the previous core belief that "all children should achieve to their full potential," a goal or priority might be, "The school organization will demonstrate growth in academic achievement by showing an overall 5% or more achievement level above the averages of demographically comparable districts over the next 2 years, as measured by the state tests in both reading and mathematics." This formulation doesn't say *how* the school is going to reach the goal; rather, it describes the target itself in clear, unambiguous, and measurable terms.

The board needs to approve both short-term and long-term goals that align to each other. But the board's responsibilities stop there, for administration and teachers should develop and implement the plans to meet such goals.

Accessing Good Data

Board access to data is crucial in determining whether the school organization is making sufficient progress toward meeting its goals or priorities. But what types of data? How much data? What should be scrutinized, and what should be ignored? If the board examines only partial data, how will the board make solid decisions? Your board needs to spend time addressing questions like these before your collection and review of data can properly inform your deliberations. Chapter 5 covers data in more detail.

Accepting the Slow Pace of Change

A school organization changes slowly. It's comparable to turning around the Queen Mary or stopping a freight train: It takes a long time to alter the organization's course. This is because any organization is a complex interaction of roles and actions, all of which need to be aligned and accounted for before a new initiative has the desired effect. Yet board members typically think the time needed for implementing a new initiative will be much shorter than what the rest of the school organization realistically needs.

Change may look easy from the elevated view of the board table: The board issues a strategic charge, and change will just happen. In fact, the tactical and operational planning, communication, and coordinated action required are anything but easy and take a significant amount of time. The most common mistake new boards make is to ignore school culture and impose new changes immediately upon being seated. Sometimes new board members feel that they've been elected with a mandate to create change. After all, children are only in a grade level for a year, and each year without change may be a "wasted" one. But if you immediately make demands for change without first taking the necessary time to learn about the school organization's culture, you will impede real progress toward the desired change rather than promote it. Administrators and teachers who are responsible for making the change happen will push back when board members ignore long-standing cultural realities, regardless of whether the desired changes are needed.

Those engaged in systems thinking break down change into measurable components and suggest realistic timeframes by which to accomplish sustained change. Successful board members accommodate their own desired pace of change to the more realistic one of the entire school organization. They push administration and operational staff to make the pace of change as fast as possible—within, not beyond, the school organization's capacity to absorb and adapt to change.

In school administration classes, prospective principals and superintendents learn to take a year to become really familiar with the school culture before trying to change it. That advice is equally appropriate for new board members: *Go slow to go fast.*

Balancing Individual Demands Against the Greater Good

Board members are beholden to two opposite constituent groups: individuals and the larger community of which they are a part. Individuals often loudly demand preferential treatment that wouldn't be good for the community as a whole, which is usually silent. As the "court of last resort," the board may not know to whom to listen: the loud and vocal individual or the "silent majority."

For example, consider a parent who doesn't like the actions of an individual teacher or principal. That parent may insist upon some sort of board or administrative retribution toward the staff person for carrying out a board policy designed for the common good. Or say that the board decides to change the starting and ending times of the school day in order to provide more time for staff development and meet improvement goals. After all, better trained teachers will benefit every child. Yet parents will view the change through the prism of their own convenience, and this particular change will be very inconvenient to them. In this example, individual dissatisfaction can easily become large-group discontent that's passionately expressed.

Understanding the Limits of Good Intentions

Every new board member is sincere in his or her desire to serve the community. Every member wants to make a positive difference for children, whether by adding to the present accomplishments of the school district or by correcting its erroneous ways. This noble stance usually assumes a big-picture, black-and-white perspective, while the board's actual work often involves the small picture, which is much more gray and nuanced than you ever anticipated.

Most boards struggle mightily to make their meeting agendas reflect their big-picture priorities and beliefs so that the organization actually changes as a result. Two realities get in the way. First, the board's work is often defined by others, as opposed to board members selecting the topics of most interest. The outside world continually interjects itself into the self-defined business of the board, limiting the board's control of even its own agendas.

Second, the board's item-by-item considerations of its agenda rarely reflect big-picture good intentions. While the impetus for service is noble, the reality of service is often regulatory, minute, and political. Given the often "small-picture" responsibilities a school board must carry out, your likelihood of receiving community thanks, much less accolades, for board service is slim.

So how do you hold onto the good intentions that drove your acceptance of board service in the first place? Good board members do hold on, and this book will explain how.

Overcoming the Tyranny of Time

There's never enough time.

First, it will take you hours to be a well-informed board member. The reading alone—agendas, background materials, reports, research, articles, and recommendations—is significant and continual. Board membership is neither for the faint of heart nor the weary of eye.

Second, the number of meetings and the time allotted for each are never enough. There will always be far more to do than possible, particularly given that most boards are restricted by open-meetings statutes that limit when, and under what conditions, members can confer with each other.

Third, even if your board feels it has had adequate time to make decisions, their scope or demands on the system may not align with the staff's abilities to carry them out—even when staff are willing to do so.

By now you may be asking, *If board service is this challenging, why should I serve?* The good news is that you can meet all of these challenges successfully; in fact, effective boards meet them regularly. This book will show you how to become the effective, strategic, and visionary team that all boards have the potential—and indeed the obligation—to be.

Chapter Summary

- There's a lot to read, know, and retrieve, because written information is the main vehicle by which you'll become fully informed in a timely fashion about issues facing the board.

- You're responsible for all children and for policies, rules, and procedures that guarantee all children are treated fairly and equally.

- You've permanently, if perhaps unknowingly, given up your "civilian" life to serve on a school board.

- You need to learn the rhythm and pace of time in the school organization before you attempt to impose your own time demands on those who implement board decisions.

- Schools are very complex businesses.

- Public schools differ from private-sector businesses in fundamental ways.

- Many educational reforms are politically based and might not align well with good educational practices.

- School changes are adjustments to complex systems that must be well thought out in advance.

- Boards must work collaboratively in order to foster change.

- Boards are always held accountable to the community they represent.

- In turn, boards must establish accountability structures within the school organization.

- Boards must act from missions, visions, and values that align to community expectations.

- Boards use goals and priorities to actualize missions, visions, and values.

- Boards must determine how they will use data to monitor the success of their goals and priorities.

- Board members must balance individual preferences with what is best for all.

- Your big-picture good intentions are at odds with the detail and complexities of real board work.

- There is never enough time for all that a board wants to accomplish.

Three Roles Essential to Every School System

One of the hardest things to get used to as a new member is that board service isn't nearly the smooth and efficient process you may have thought it would be, especially if in your professional life, you were the creator of (or at least part of) an efficient, well-oiled business, organization, or home. You and other board members will spend a lot of time simply organizing how your board is going to spend its time, and it will seem that no one completely "owns" the entire process.

That's because no one does. Neither a board nor the school district staff can achieve their individual ends without the support of the other. A board works in *collaboration* with school district staff, especially the superintendent, who is the board's proxy in directing and deploying staff.

It all begins to make sense when we consider the necessarily different roles of the board and of school time management and resource procurement and allocation.

Understanding the Strategic, Tactical, and Operational Roles

A school board serves a *strategic* role. In this role, the board considers the "big picture," the 50,000-foot view. It looks years into the future, taking a broad view that spans the entire organization and represents the entire community. A school board at its best is a visionary, strategic change agent.

A strategic change agent doesn't directly make change happen, but rather sets a strategic *charge* or target for change that others have to reach. The board considers what the school district needs to make changes in an aligned and efficient way over many years. It keeps administrators focused on those changes and helps ensure the availability of the resources required to make them, but doesn't manage the more medium-term tactics that will bring them about. Finally, as a strategic change agent, the board takes a positive stance toward change, viewing it as something that makes an organization better.

School administration assumes a *tactical* role, which isn't quite as broad as the big picture; it's the 10,000-foot view. This is a somewhat detailed and narrower perspective that typically looks 1 to 3 years into the future and understands the organization in terms of schools, grades, and classes. As a tactical change agent, administration focuses on constituent groups: parents, students, and educational staff. Tactical change agents create and deploy plans to meet the strategic charge set by the board.

But although school administrators want to positively affect children's learning, they can only indirectly do so through developing plans that teachers carry out. Teachers assume an *operational* role, which is a "small-picture," ground-level view that is highly detailed and focuses on daily, weekly, and occasional monthly instructional units. Teachers alone have direct access to children, usually in the classroom or, less often, through a teaching team. As operational change agents, teachers take the tactical plan and refine it so it will actually change the way children receive instruction in their classrooms. If everything is in alignment, teachers' operational adjustments, filtered through the administration's tactical plan, will meet the board's strategic targets.

Table 2-1 summarizes the definitions of the three roles.

Table 2-1: Strategic, Tactical, and Operational Definitions

Strategic	Tactical	Operational
Sees the big picture—the 50,000-foot view	Sees the wide picture—the 10,000-foot view	Focuses on the small picture—is the point of impact with children
Overlooks the entire school organization and sees how the parts relate to the whole	Coordinates the component parts of the organization	Coordinates a specific part of the organization
Focuses on representing the community's needs and interests	Overlooks schools and departments	Overlooks a classroom, department, or teaching team
Looks to the long term, usually 3–5 years	Focuses on working with constituent groups (parents, students, and staff)	Focuses primarily on the students
Provides overall structure at a district-goals level	Looks 1–3 years ahead into the future	Looks days, weeks, months, or, at most, 1 year into the future
Sets clear targets for improvement	Provides structure at district and school levels	Provides detailed structure at a classroom level
	Creates and deploys plans that will lead to improvement	Refines and adjusts plans, so that improvement will result

Three issues define the different roles played by the board, administration, and teachers:

1. Expertise

2. Time

3. Access

Expertise

Each role has areas of expertise that the others don't share. The school organization is like a car going to a distant spot beyond the horizon. The strategists determine that spot. The tacticians then drive the car; they develop a map, a timeline, and a plan for how to reach the spot on the horizon. They also choose the proper roads and make sure that the car is in good operating condition and has plenty of gas. Finally, the operationalists are the vehicle itself—the components that work together to take all the passengers along the chosen route to reach the destination. Nothing will happen, despite a destination and a roadmap to get there, if the car isn't in shape to run efficiently for a long time.

Board members are district strategists. They are in the most competent and capable role to set strategic charges and organizational direction; they're not directly beholden to staff relationships and institutional habits, and so can focus cleanly on how the school organization serves students. As community members and taxpayers, they directly represent the community the school organization serves. They are superbly qualified to address long-term vision and strategies.

Administrators are district tacticians. They craft plans to carry out the board's strategic charges within a school organization culture and setting. They have the best view of the school organization in all its detail and understand its cultural idiosyncrasies. This makes them experts in gauging the potential for change, and as only administrators are legally certificated to promote change through evaluating staff performance, they are the most likely of the three roles to successfully combine and deploy resources to address the board's strategic charges. Only tacticians have the time and access to resources to promote and bring about change in a standardized way across the entire school organization.

Teachers are district operationalists. They alone can directly reach students through instruction; neither strategists nor tacticians can do so, no matter how committed they are or how hard they try. Even if they could, they don't have the instructional qualifications and skill sets to have the impact that teachers have. Classroom expertise begins and ends with teachers. *The farther a role operates from the classroom itself, the greater its capacity to think big and the lesser its ability to* directly *change anything that really matters.* To operate effectively, teachers need clear instructional targets, proper training and instructional materials, assistance with children who need more individualized help, and assessment checkpoints.

These three roles are interdependent. To return to the car analogy, we need a destination, a travel plan, and a car that runs efficiently to successfully complete a journey; so, too, must the three roles act in a well-synchronized way for meaningful organizational change to occur. No two roles can effect change without the third. This creates a virtual mandate for an organizational commitment to collaboration.

Time

The board, administration, and teachers view time very differently.

Because board members are the farthest removed from the classroom and often don't understand its operational realities, they see the potential for classroom change as occurring at a quicker pace than do the other two roles. By nature, they're usually in a hurry—they often have or know children in the system, so time is of the essence to them. Although their strategic role requires board members to address long-term, often multiyear goals, they want to see things "moving along" and will typically push tacticians to figure out ways to keep things progressing ever faster. The irony is that board members have primary responsibility for long-term goals that cover long *spans* of time, but have a quickened *sense* of the time required to commit change.

With teachers, this sense of time is exactly the opposite; they deal with shorter spans of time and perceive the pace of change to be very slow. Remember that a teacher's world is measured in daily lesson plans and weekly or monthly instructional plans. Children arrive at the classroom every day, and a good teacher has to be prepared for them. Because the pressure to be ready is so constant and intense, teachers don't easily think in terms of developing and adding new things to their already-full plates. In fact, it's a considerable challenge for teachers just to keep up with what they're already doing, so they're less likely to embrace the changes that boards are in a hurry to implement.

As tacticians, administrators bridge this gap between expectation and reality. A central task of administration is to negotiate realistic timeframes for change that still move things along. Administrators set the plans to meet the strategic charges of the board. The development and implementation of these plans might take a year or more. But because administrators need to spell out the steps needed to achieve the goals the board has set, they think in terms of how long each step will take and how each step fits into the plan's overall timeline. In so doing, they try to balance the board's need to speed things up with the teacher's natural instinct to slow things down. They know the board will push to implement a plan as soon as possible and that teachers will push back because of their day to-day obligations. And administrators also know that even if they craft a beautiful plan, that won't matter if the plan doesn't result in improved student-teacher interaction in the classroom.

Access

The board, administration, and teachers must all acknowledge where change matters most: in the classroom, with students. All must understand how to work within the structure of the school organization to have the greatest effect on the classroom level.

By virtue of their operational role, teachers have direct access to students, so they have the greatest potential to make change happen. But because of their time constraints, they're the least likely to *initiate* systemic change. While individual teachers may make changes that benefit their students—good teachers do so all the time—these changes are not systemic, and therefore most of their colleagues don't even know about such changes (much less adopt them in their own classrooms).

As tacticians, administrators are one step removed from directly implementing classroom change. While they don't have direct access to students, they do have access to teachers, and can indirectly affect the experiences students have by changing how teachers use their time. No matter how elegantly designed their tactical plans for change, if administrators can't get teachers to buy into them, no meaningful change will result.

As strategists, board members are two-and-a-half steps removed from directly implementing classroom change. They have direct access to the superintendent, who has direct access to administration, which in turn has direct access to teachers, who have direct access to students. Though the board may be in the biggest hurry to make change happen, it is the furthest removed from the point of action.

This chain of access is a constant that can't be altered—it is a fundamental reality that every school board must accept to be effective. No matter how passionate, creative, or committed your board is, you'll always be two-and-a-half steps removed from being able to directly implement meaningful change. Failure to understand this reality frequently results in a board micromanaging administration.

Table 2-2 (page 18) summarizes the three essential roles.

Avoiding Micromanagement

Micromanagement occurs when a person in one role tries to assume the functions and responsibilities of someone in another role. It's the opposite of role alignment, in which each person works in a coordinated fashion with others, including those in different roles, to achieve common goals or priorities.

School staff often accuse boards or board members of micromanagement—typically when a board goes beyond its strategic role of setting goals and tries to make or implement plans to carry out those goals, a tactical process that belongs to administration.

Administrators also can micromanage, as when they try to dictate (as opposed to recommend) goals or priorities to a board, or when they fail to account for operational constraints in trying to implement plans. Even teachers can micromanage when they simply refuse to try a new tactical plan rather than work with administration to make the plan reflect classroom realities.

Micromanaging slows or halts momentum and saps energy. It also creates parallel and competing efforts to accomplish the same thing, and pits roles against each other instead of leveraging them toward collaborative efforts.

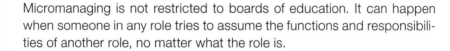

Micromanaging is not restricted to boards of education. It can happen when someone in any role tries to assume the functions and responsibilities of another role, no matter what the role is.

Micromanaging increases the workload for everyone. *When roles are out of alignment, everyone works harder and feels more frustrated, while actually getting less done.* Like a car that is badly out of tune, the system can still run, but it has to work much harder, wears out parts faster, and performs less efficiently. Mileage goes down, and the need for repairs goes up.

Micromanaging means that the *position* rather than the *role* is allowed to define expertise; a person thinks his or her position as a board member trumps the experience and role-based expertise of another individual.

This is an easy trap for board members in particular to fall into, because most bring some real tactical knowledge to the board table—most board members want to serve on the board to put their professional and personal skills to the service of the community's schools. But the board role calls for strategic, not tactical, skills.

Administrators already have the necessary tactical skill sets and have the distinct advantage of having practiced those skill sets in *school settings,* usually for a long time. In contrast, board members have to learn a whole new set of strategic skills.

Table 2-2: Strategic, Tactical, and Operational Roles

Role	Expertise	Time	Access
Strategists	Directly represent the community Are focused on how the organization serves its "customers"—families and students Are superbly qualified to address long-term mission, vision, values, and goals of the district	See the potential for quick change in smaller increments of time, even though they set long-term goals that span several years Feel that time is of the essence Want to see things "moving along"	Have direct access to the superintendent Are furthest removed from the ability to make change happen Can't begin systemic change on their own
Tacticians	Have direct influence on staff performance Are focused on the use of resources to create and implement plans in a standardized way Are certified to improve staff performance	Have time horizons that are shorter than those of strategists but longer than those of operationalists Negotiate realistic timeframes with operational staff Think in terms of how much time each step needed to implement a plan will take	Have direct access to staff Must get staff to buy into a proposed change in order to sustain meaningful change over time Are not likely to induce systemic change on their own
Operationalists	Exercise direct influence on instruction of students Are focused on the growth of individual students Are qualified and certified to improve student achievement	See the potential for change in longer increments of time Believe that time is precious and there is a lot to do to be ready, let alone to address change	Have direct access to students Can most directly make classroom change happen Are least likely to induce systemic change on their own

Micromanagement feels personal and visceral. We feel bad—even antagonized—when our advice and expertise are rejected or discounted. Yet when you understand that your responsibilities as a board member are defined by your role within the broader organization, you'll realize that what is happening isn't personal at all.

Creating Systemic Alignment

The board's role in the decision-making process is crucial, because if a board doesn't set strategic charges, no one else will, and changes will be sporadic, random, un-aligned, and temporary—even as workloads, decisions regarding resource priorities, and strife increase. In fact, that is the perfect description of a school organization that is out of systemic alignment.

Systemic alignment occurs when the entire school organization works toward common organizational goals in mutually supportive ways. This becomes a much more complicated and difficult task when individual initiatives compete with common organizational goals. That's because individual initiatives tend to create their own demands and thereby draw time and resources away from common organizational goals. An example is a language arts program that is carried out differently in every school in the district, with different instructional materials, different learning expectations, and different student assessments. Each school's implementation of language arts forms its own set of resource and time commitments that has to be supported by the organization. But because each school carries out its language arts program differently, there's no common way to measure results at a district level and no overall district efficiency in either the cost or training required to support multiple language arts approaches. This creates initiative "silos"—initiatives that stand much like silos on a farm, unconnected to each other—which then compete for organizational time and resources.

Clearly, the board can't manage the tactical and operational details required for systemic alignment, as outlined in Table 2-2 (page 18). However, the board can conceive of and drive a vision of systemic alignment for the entire school organization by doing the following:

- Demanding an overall strategic plan for the school organization—a plan informed by parent, student, community, and staff perspectives

- Establishing goals or priorities that support each other rather than compete for time and resources

- Charging the administration to determine whether the school organization's resource allocation practices—distribution of people, time, and money—are aligned with the organization's goals and priorities

- Directing the administration to limit initiatives to those that align with the organization's goals and priorities

- Ensuring that all board-authorized staff development and training are aligned with those goals and priorities

- Pushing for outcomes-based goals, but only after needed process-based goals are firmly in place

- Using data to measure whether significant changes have occurred and what the benefits are to children

- Requiring that administration develop benchmarks for comparing data to measure change

A Strategic Plan

- Sets goals and priorities
- Aligns actions and behaviors
- Charges administration to:
  + Align spending habits.
  + Limit initiatives to those that align with goals and priorities.
  + Change process-based goals to outcome-based goals.
- Uses data to monitor progress to:
  + Ensure that significant changes are occurring and that benefits are accruing for children as a result

Combining clear goals with consistent measurement of outcomes and aligned leadership and employee behaviors throughout the organization will drive results and accelerate improvement.

> A board needs to put its primary energies and efforts into promoting systemic alignment if it is to supply the vision that every *successful* school organization must have.

Building Bridges Across Roles

People serve as formal and informal bridges to connect the roles we've been discussing. Some positions in the school system are *formal* bridges designed to serve as links between roles. *Informal* bridges are created when people assume the responsibilities of another role in a purposeful and mutually acceptable way.

Formal Bridges

There are three formal bridges in any school organization: the superintendent, the principal, and the staff labor organization. (For our purposes, we'll call this group "the union.")

The Superintendent

The school superintendent, or an equivalent title, serves as the formal bridge between strategic and tactical roles by working intimately with the board and administration. In decision-making, the superintendent's role is to see that tactical plans are created and carried out to meet the board's strategic charges—and he or she is accountable for the results. The superintendent builds execution into the organization's strategy, goals, and culture. The superintendent can't set a strategic charge, though the superintendent can, and often does, submit information and make recommendations that lead to strategic board decisions.

Information and recommendations can flow the other way, too. Individual board members or the board as a whole can make tactical recommendations to a superintendent, but only the superintendent has the authority to approve such recommendations for implementation. Information in the form of recommendations can flow freely in both directions as long as recommendations are not mistaken for directives or demands.

The Principal

The principal serves as the formal bridge between administration's tactical and faculty's operational roles. The principal is responsible for implementing tactical plans, but must take into account the operational realities of teachers and other school staff, particularly given the close physical proximity within a school of teachers to the principal. Information will flow back and forth between them, though not always directly or efficiently, because the line between tactical and operational needs is often murky and must be continually renegotiated. Though the principal is subject to the tactical plan of the superintendent and the overall administration, teachers may erroneously perceive the principal as being the plan's author and may assume he or she has decision-making authority over the plan.

The Union

The union is the third bridge. It links the operational and tactical levels, usually through contractual discussions. Union leaders may confront principals and other management when they feel management is making unfair or inappropriate demands that the staff contract doesn't allow. The union also can serve as an operational-strategic bridge by interacting with a school board during the collective bargaining process.

In an aligned school organization, the union serves as a working partner, not an adversary. The union calls attention to the operational realities and concerns so that all three roles can collaborate effectively in achieving strategic goals. This may sound like a pipedream to board members who are used to an adversarial relationship with unions, but it can in fact occur. When it does, the union can communicate with staff about systematic changes far more effectively than can board members, superintendents, or administrators.

In a collaborative board-administration-union relationship, the three parties share their unique perspectives, but no party tells the other two what to decide; instead, they tell each other what to *avoid* in order that the mutually desired end result can be achieved. The relationship among the three roles changes from adversarial to collaborative when they pursue a powerful common goal: to ensure the best education for children. School organizations that continue to have adversarial relationships are choosing to fight rather than to improve. No organization can fight *and* improve.

Informal Bridges

Informal bridges are created when a person in one role assumes some of the duties of another role, but the decision to do so is mutual and comfortable for all concerned. For example, a board member who is an engineer can lend expertise to a school construction project. When the administrator responsible for the project doesn't possess expertise in this area, and when he or she works well with the board member, the board member–engineer can appropriately offer technical expertise and advice.

The line between appropriate and inappropriate involvement lies in the manner of the interaction, not the quality of expertise offered. A good board member is equally willing to supply expertise if asked *and* to refrain from doing so if told that other expertise is already available. If accepted by the administrator, the board member's offer to become, in effect, a free technical consultant can benefit everyone. But if a board member foists himself or herself into discussions of tactics against the administrator's wishes—even if unexpressed (a superintendent or principal may be loath to stand up to an insistent board member)—the "help" is inappropriate micromanagement.

Implementing a Collaborative Decision-Making Cycle

So how do these three roles—strategic, tactical, and operational—mesh productively?

What's needed is a decision-making cycle to align the three roles in making and carrying out decisions. Figure 2-1 illustrates this five-step process, which starts and ends with the board's strategic charge. In the middle lies the work of tactical and operational staff in addressing that board's strategic charge.

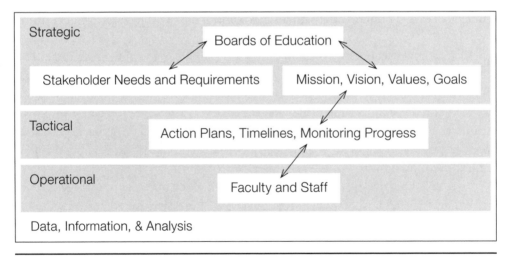

Figure 2-1: There are five steps in the decision-making cycle.

Step 1

The first step is for the board to craft a strategic charge from the school district's goals and priorities. *Board goals* and *district goals* should, for now, be considered interchangeable, as the board is the strategic role expert; its goals should be the school organization's goals and vice versa. The charge should be specific enough to give clear direction but broad enough to allow for tactical and operational adjustments. A board charge generally concerns either process or outcome.

A *process* charge might be "to formulate a plan to increase the rigor of instruction for high-end learners across all grade levels." The charge is to create a plan, not to assess how it actually works. An *outcomes* charge might be "to increase the rigor of instruction for high-end learners across all grade levels." An outcomes charge indicates an expectation of classroom change, thus the degree of classroom change will have to be measured to determine to what extent the charge has been met. The board must first create an infrastructure for systemic change through process charges; then it issues outcomes charges to embed the changes permanently throughout the school organization.

In conceptualizing and setting a strategic charge, the board can gain knowledge and insights from many sources, including staff, community members, advisory committees, and research literature. However, the charge should align to the board's mission, vision, values, and goals, so that it becomes part of a systemic approach to change to which everyone is committed.

Step 2

The second step in the decision-making cycle is for the administrators to develop a tactical plan, including specific steps and a timeline to carry them out. This is the step at which boards are most likely to micromanage; resist the temptation! Let administration formulate the plan, even in an area where you have personal talent and relevant experience. Remember, no matter how good your tactical experiences have been, they probably weren't *educational* experiences, much less tactical experiences in your *particular school organization*. Knowing the organizational culture and local tactical considerations is critical to successful change efforts. The administration's plan, whatever it may be, will have to align to and be guided by your board's charge.

Step 3

The third step is to seek staff feedback on the tactical plan. Administrators at the 10,000-foot perspective must go to the people who are "on the ground" to check their plan against operational realities. Usually, they learn that the timeline is too short for staff development and implementation on the classroom level, perhaps because teachers are already managing other initiatives that will compete with the new plan.

Step 4

The fourth step is an informal negotiation between the tactical and operational levels to meet staff needs without slowing the plan's implementation to a crawl. This nitty-gritty time reveals the school organization's capacity to adapt to change. The results of the discussion between administration and staff may be far removed from the board's original timeframe for its strategic charge. But this type of negotiation is clearly one that a board is ill-suited to hold, for only the staff can credibly discuss intra-staff issues.

Step 5

The final step brings the board back into the decision-making process. Now the plan—tactically designed by administration and operationally vetted by teachers—comes back to the board, which considers whether the plan still meets its original charge. After all, the tactical and operational levels don't have the right to change a board's strategic charge, but instead are obliged to design and carry out a plan that meets that charge. So a board must reconsider its original charge and determine whether the new plan developed in response is satisfactory. If the board agrees that it is, then the plan is ready for implementation. If not, the charge is restated with further clarity, and Steps 2, 3, and 4 begin anew.

> Decision-making is like an insurance premium on time: You can pay a little up front, or you can pay more later. Either way, a bill comes due.

The decision-making cycle takes time, particularly when it has to be repeated because the strategic charge and the original plan weren't aligned. Yet all the time taken is ultimately worth it if positive change occurs.

Shared Decision-Making

Now that we understand the different roles played by board members, administration, and school staff, we can see that confusion about roles often lies at the heart of organizational misunderstandings. Understanding and aligning roles are especially important when it comes to making decisions.

In some well-known models of *shared decision-making,* such as win-win bargaining or interest-based negotiation, different roles exercise their relative strengths and communicate their perceptions and insights about an issue to come to a commonly accepted decision. Expertise is assumed to be common across all parties, even if not always in equal measure. The sensitive nature of the content being negotiated drives any collaboration that occurs, not an acknowledged need for different expertise across roles. In this case, the parties commit to shared decision-making because they believe collaboration is the right thing to do. This process may result in good decisions, but the *quality* of the decision is often perceived as secondary to the importance of a collaborative *process* to reach consensus.

Once we acknowledge role expertise, however, shared decision-making becomes more than just a good intention or a choice of style; it becomes an essential process for making the *best* decision. All three roles are *required* to participate in order to make that best decision because each brings an essential strategic, tactical, or operational perspective. Pooling expertise means that all parties realize that no one or two roles can arrive at the best decision by themselves. Issues are therefore not debated, but aligned. Of course, an up-front acknowledgment of role expertise does not guarantee the right decision will be made, but it's far more likely to do so.

Site-based decision-making brings the shared decision-making process to the school level. While districtwide goals define targets for the entire organization, site goals narrow the targets to each school's specific needs. Teachers at each site help formulate these goals; it stands to reason that those who directly access children should have a significant say in what and how children are taught. Board members probably won't be aware of differences in the specific skills each individual school must improve to reach the shared organizational goal.

For example, a goal for the school organization might be to raise the percentage of children who score in the top two levels of the state tests for reading. Based upon the school's state achievement test data results, a site goal for Elementary School A might be to try to meet this target by focusing on extended written responses to test questions (these require a more detailed understanding than multiple-choice questions) because its achievement data showed that this area in reading was its lowest achieving area as a school. Given different achievement test data results, Elementary School B might focus upon reading-comprehension questions (these assess whether a student can select the most important detail from a passage). Both schools are helping children gain higher level skills that fall under the school organization's goal, but each creates a plan specific to the site's particular needs.

While the board sets an overall target, school staff knows they can't address all areas of need simultaneously. As a result, they must select an area of need based on a detailed analysis of what is most important for their school, and which is aligned with the school organization's goals, and can be measured and documented.

> The organization, and each school within it, has a finite capacity for change. What any school can address at a given time must be culled from a much larger potential list of things that could all benefit from change. That selection process belongs at the site level—not at the board table— as long as what is chosen still addresses the board's overall goal.

A significant problem occurs when either the board wants to micromanage the site targets for improvement, or the site wants to focus its energies on something that has little to do with the board's goals. In such instances, the board and the site aren't aligned with each other's needs and roles. Strategists cannot set goals at the site level as well as the professionals at that site can. In turn, operational staff need to select goals that align with broader board goals for the overall benefit of the entire school organization.

Building a School System, Not a System of Schools

It is more effective to be a *school system* than a *system of schools*. A *school system* is aligned across the entire organization—vertically, from "top to bottom" across roles, and horizontally in terms of initiatives that don't compete with each other for time and resources. The reverse, a *system of schools,* operates with schools independent of—rather than aligned with—each other and the overall goals of the school organization.

A school system is focused and efficient; its staff maximizes time and resources toward meeting the school organization's goals. A system of schools is haphazard and random; although isolated schools may accomplish good things, the overall school organization doesn't change in a focused, continuous way.

Table 2-3 summarizes the differences between the two systems.

Table 2-3: School System Versus System of Schools

School System	System of Schools
Aligned across the entire organization, vertically across roles, and horizontally in terms of initiatives	Comprised of schools that are independent of—rather than aligned with—each other and with the school organization's goals
Uses shared decision-making based on role expertise	Concerned more with individual or school initiatives
Sets goals and priorities that don't compete with each other for time and resources	Characterized by competing initiatives
Characterized by focused and efficient alignment; use of time and resources is maximized to meet organizational and school goals	Marked by haphazard and random alignment that doesn't change the overall organization in a focused, continuous way

The school organization must make a strategic decision to be a school system rather than a system of schools. This decision requires formal board approval and support because it has significant implications for the use of the school organization's time and resources.

Applying Your Strategic Role

The key to staying strategically on track is to understand the distinctions among *recommending, deciding,* and *implementing* policy. Four areas where a board exercises strategic responsibilities, and might be tempted to move into the tactical area assumed by administrators, are:

1. Policy development

2. Evaluation of the superintendent

3. Evaluation of other staff

4. Assessment of programs

Exceptions to the Strategic Role

A board of education cannot always remain in a strictly strategic role. Laws and mandates in most states sometimes require a board to take tactical or even operational actions, such as:

- Approval of specific pay orders
- Monthly line-item budget reviews
- Final determinations on the suspension or expulsion of students
- Serving in a hearing capacity during due process on disciplinary matters
- Participation or leadership in collective bargaining contract negotiations
- Formal action on the hiring or dismissal of employees
- The evaluation of the superintendent and determination of his or her salary and benefits package
- Approval of textbooks

The board must not ignore its mandated legal duties, but it must still maintain its strategic perspective. In instances like these, the board, although legally empowered to carry out legislative mandates through a public vote, should rely heavily upon its administrative staff. That staff firmly understands the tactical and operational considerations involved and thus might possess more expertise to guide the board's decisions. (The one exception to this concerns the board's exclusive prerogative to evaluate and set the superintendent's salary.) When a board decides to disregard the professional staff's recommendation, it should have very good and well thought out reasons for doing so.

Policy Development

When there is a perceived need for a policy addition or modification, either board members or tactical staff (usually the superintendent) can initiate a back-and-forth discussion to draft a new policy for board approval.

The responsibility for the actual writing of this draft belongs to tactical staff due to the needs to apply policy to the actual work environment and to meet timelines for preparing policy-oriented materials for board meetings. Even if a board member is an accomplished wordsmith, he or she likely won't be aware of such workplace nuances as negotiated contract implications or legally mandated restrictions, much less the schedule that's required to bring drafts forward to the whole board in a timely manner. In contrast, tactical staff regularly addresses such requirements as part of their daily routines and responsibilities. However, a board should still exercise its strategic role of setting and approving policy for the school organization by maintaining editorial control of the draft. Only a board, by majority vote, can approve the final policy.

Evaluation of the Superintendent

This is the only staff evaluation for which a board is directly responsible. The superintendent is the only formal bridge between the strategic and tactical role, so a significant part of his or her responsibility is to assist the board in formulating strategic charges and to provide background information and data for board decision-making. The board is in the best position to evaluate how well the superintendent fulfills that role.

However, the board has direct knowledge of only half of what the superintendent does; the other half consists of the tactical measures that he or she employs with staff to carry out board charges. But the board can indirectly judge the success of those tactics based upon how well its strategic charges are carried out.

Evaluation criteria for the superintendent should be aligned to the school district goals, just as everything in a true school system should be. This means that in evaluating the superintendent's tactics, a board is primarily concerned with how well he or she supports and carries out the board's strategic charges. Such alignment guarantees that the evaluation process will be professional, respectful, and based on objective, measurable criteria. (This doesn't, however, preclude a board from setting a qualitative strategic charge, such as "to achieve high staff morale," that can be measured through survey instruments.)

This focus on alignment orients the evaluation process toward goal achievement as opposed to a "gotcha" mentality, whereby a board waits to catch the superintendent making a mistake. It also places the responsibility squarely on the superintendent's shoulders to manage resources so as to help accomplish school organization goals. There are no acceptable explanations that "something else was more important" unless the board and superintendent jointly decide that an especially challenging matter requires shifting organizational priorities.

What makes this evaluation process work? The answer is all in the timing. Most boards spend the bulk of the evaluation process at the end of the school year, and the evaluation often becomes little more than a recitation of the things that board members have most keenly and recently felt about the superintendent. This process rarely takes the superintendent's performance during the entire school year into account and can seem subjective. The result is usually disappointing and unsatisfactory for both the board and the superintendent.

In an aligned evaluation process, the real work is done at the *beginning* of the school year, when the board sets specific, reasonable, measurable goals for the superintendent. A board should know what it wants to see changed, but the superintendent has to define and manage the ability of the organization to respond effectively. Discussions around those goals take place throughout the school year between the board president (or a board committee) and the superintendent. At the end of the school year, there are no surprises; instead of a lengthy and stressful process, the board and superintendent simply wrap up what has been taking place all along.

The board and the superintendent work together, synchronizing their perspectives to develop reasonable goals that will move the school organization forward.

The board issues a charge to what it wants to see changed, while the superintendent defines the organization's realistic abilities to respond effectively to that charge. If that occurs, the board's assessment of the superintendent won't come as a surprise; if it does, then the evaluation process has failed its litmus test of proceeding according to aligned goals.

Evaluation of Other Staff

This item is simple. It's not the board's role to assess any staff other than the superintendent. No other staff members interface directly with the board. In fact, most states require professional certifications to evaluate public education staff, a requirement that keeps boards, among others, from doing so. The board can evaluate how well the superintendent assigns, utilizes, and leverages performance of other staff—and the board can *recommend* to the superintendent its views on the performance of staff, particularly administrative staff—but it's the responsibility of the superintendent and other certified administrators to evaluate the performance of other staff.

A common example of how this process can go wrong is when the board ends up directing the superintendent to fire the football coach, either because the team has a consistently losing record or because certain parents complain about why their child isn't a starting member of the team or object to the coach's personal style or game strategy. For the board to order the firing of the coach would be to step out of its strategic and into a tactical evaluative role for which it's unqualified. Yet what is the alternative for the board that feels the coach really *is* failing to carry out the job properly? The board can report its dissatisfaction to the superintendent and, guided by him or her, charge the administration to develop some realistic performance expectations by which the coach can be evaluated during the next year. The performance expectations need to account for the issues swirling around the coach, but should do so through a professional, objective evaluation process. In this way, then, the board can express its dissatisfaction through recommendations of evaluative criteria to the superintendent without superseding the administration's evaluative role.

> An aligned evaluation process doesn't address whether a staff member is popular or unpopular, liked or disliked, haughty or humble, or on the right or the wrong side of an issue. None of that matters, unless it is the reason that the school organization didn't attain one of its goals. When subjective criteria are used, the evaluation process becomes unprofessional and unaligned.

The board's role in staff assessment is solely to keep its eye on the school organization's goals and to judge through objective data how well those goals are being met. Although the board does not "do" staff evaluations, the board does have the final say on staffing recommendations brought by administration—for example, with regard to granting teacher tenure. The board doesn't assess a teacher's eligibility for tenure; it only *grants* tenure once administrators have assessed such eligibility. Similarly, the board does not set salary raises (other than for the superintendent). Rather, it should set guidelines for how much to be spent on staff as a whole as well as for what generally constitutes acceptable performance. In short, the board's role is to set standards for roles at an organizational level, not to evaluate individuals who fill those roles.

The board can publicly define the level of rigor that the administration should follow in its evaluation process and insist that the administration receive board approval for that process, as in the football coach example. The board has the right to expect that the staff evaluation process is aligned throughout the system and that evaluation supports attaining goals. When the board exercises this kind of authority, particularly when it's guided by the strategic goals it has set, it has a powerful indirect influence on how the superintendent and his or her administrative team will address staffing needs.

Assessment of Programs

The board doesn't directly assess the educational programs in its schools. But it should elicit information and observations from the superintendent on how well existing programs meet the school organization's goals.

Because board members assume a strategic role and usually aren't educators themselves, they're in a poor position to objectively assess an educational program's effectiveness. But the programs' outcomes, as reflected in student achievement data that reveal the degree of progress toward meeting school organization goals, are fair game for board questioning. The board doesn't so much assess educational programs as it challenges school staff to justify their effectiveness.

For example, if a school organization wants to purchase a new reading series, the administration (tactical level) formulates a plan to identify the right reading series, and teachers (the operational level) consider the options generated by the search process and provide feedback about each series' likelihood of success in the classroom. The board must approve before the school organization can purchase the proposed reading series. But you should do this only after the administration convinces you that the search for a new series was thorough and the choice justified—not based on how individual members feel about the reading series.

This attention to a predetermined level of rigor is the board's strategic contribution to a tactical and operational process. The board defines the rigor of the assessment, but creates neither the process for assessment nor its outcomes. The board's involvement in the first and last stages of the decision-making cycle is crucial, but indirect.

Maintaining Your Strategic Focus

You may have joined a school board in the first place because you've been a successful tactician and problem-solver in your professional or home experience. Now you want the opportunity to take the skills that you have developed elsewhere to the level of public service. Remember, however, that the school organization already has a full set of tacticians—principals and administrators—who often are as skilled in their setting as you are in your home or business. The school organization doesn't need "competing" tacticians, but that's sometimes what it gets, especially with inexperienced boards.

This isn't to say that your past tactical successes are irrelevant. But if the board immerses itself in tactics, not only are board members jockeying for the same tactical responsibilities filled by administration, but they are also leaving the strategic needs of the school organization unattended.

For example, the board sets an appropriately strategic charge if it directs the administration to create timelines and steps to reach the school organization's goals. The board can then monitor progress toward meeting those goals. However, the board acts inappropriately if it determines its own timelines and step sequences, and then dictates the reporting format that it wants tactical staff to use. That's micromanaging.

Why would the board micromanage? Because board members have many tactical skills; they are simply doing what they've done successfully in the past. Translating tactical into strategic skill sets isn't difficult, once you realize that translation is required. After all, the same qualities—intelligence, perception, problem-solving abilities, analytical skills, understanding of organizational culture, and planning abilities—are as necessary for good strategic decisions as they are for good tactical ones.

Consider, for example, that if you became a member of a hospital board of directors, you wouldn't assume that you could assist the doctor in making a medical diagnosis (the tactical role) or could help him or her during surgery (the operational role). Why? Because medical professionals have been trained in skills that are specific to their tasks, while you know you lack that training (even if you're an avid viewer of TV programs on doctors and hospitals). Similarly, educators have been trained in skills needed for their tasks, and unless you're a licensed educator, you don't have that training, either. Even if you *are* a licensed educator, your board role will make the school staff question your involvement in tactics or operations because you're operating from a strategic perspective, not a tactical or operational perspective.

Again, if the board and administrators compete to control tactics, no one will assume the strategic responsibilities the school organization requires. Two competing tactical groups means that neither will be efficient. Remember that the board is two-and-a-half steps removed from being able to directly affect what children experience in classrooms, while the administration is only one step removed from being able to do so—and therefore has a far better view of the operational and cultural impediments to change.

The next chapter will discuss how the board creates structures and communication processes to manage roles and achieve its goals efficiently.

Chapter Summary

Understanding the Strategic, Tactical, and Operational Roles

- School boards are strategic experts and set strategic charges.

- Administrators have tactical expertise; teachers have operational expertise.

- All three areas of expertise must be aligned for meaningful organizational change to occur.

- Each role sees and utilizes time differently.

- Educational change depends on access, on what will actually change the learning experiences of children.

Avoiding Micromanagement

- Micromanaging occurs when one role tries to assume the functions and responsibilities of another.

- The opposite of micromanagement is role alignment, when all roles work in coordination for common ends.

- The typical trigger for micromanagement occurs when a situation (rather than a role) is allowed to determine expertise.

Creating Systemic Alignment

- Only the board is responsible for setting strategic charges.

- Systemic alignment is when the entire organization, at every role level, commits to common organizational goals within mutually supportive ways.

- A good strategic plan is a roadmap for systemic alignment.

Building Bridges Across Roles

- Superintendents bridge the gap between strategies and tactics; principals and teachers unions bridge the gap between tactics and operations.

- Appropriate informal bridges occur when both parties agree, without coercion, that situational expertise trumps role expertise.

Implementing a Collaborative Decision-Making Cycle

- The cycle aligns the three roles in creating and carrying out effective decisions.

- Board charges can be either process-based or outcomes-based.

- Key process-based goals must be met before outcomes-based goals can be effectively addressed.

- Collaboration based on role expertise should drive shared decision-making.

- Site goals are school-formulated goals that align to larger organizational goals.

- Individual schools, not the board, should establish site goals, but such targets should always align to school organization goals.

Building a School System, Not a System of Schools

- A school system aligns across the entire district, vertically across roles, and horizontally in terms of initiatives that compete for time and resources.

- In a system of schools, sites operate independently of each other and the school organization.

Applying Your Strategic Role

- Four applications—policy development, evaluation of the superintendent, evaluation of other staff, and assessment of programs—illustrate the authority and limits of the strategic role.

Maintaining Your Strategic Focus

- Most board members come to the board with tactical expertise and experiences but must learn their new role is strategic.

- Don't compete with administration over who will be in charge of tactics.

Communication Is Key

If being efficient means the school board can act as it sees fit and not worry about anyone affected by its decisions, then serving on the board is anything but, given the legal, political, and practical constraints on the board's actions. Because of these constraints, it's more important how the board conducts its business than what that business is. The most critical part concerns how, when, and why the board communicates with tactical, operational, parent, and community groups, all of whose support your board will need to provide strategic leadership.

Communication takes care and time, which you must build into the board's working schedule. Many boards will find they spend more time—and more productive time—communicating the background to and reasons for their decisions than they will making them. That may seem counterintuitive, but any successful leader knows that decisions alone change nothing. *People* change things, but only if decisions are communicated to them in ways that they can understand and relate to. Thus, the key to board leadership is your ability to persuasively *communicate* decisions, not just the power to make them. As the strategic leader of a school district, your board needs to communicate so that individuals in various roles can understand, relate to, and carry out the board's strategic decisions.

In particular, the board and the superintendent can't communicate with each other too often or too well. Much of what they need to discuss is process: how to ensure that each group stays within its role and supports the other in its role. Process communications require a collaborative relationship. In fact, this collaboration is absolutely necessary to the smooth operation of the school organization.

 An aligned approach that avoids the pitfalls of tactical competition depends upon two commitments by both board and administration: communication and collaboration.

The amount of time spent communicating rather than doing might seem counterintuitive at first. Each role has many important things to accomplish: programs to implement, initiatives to craft, test scores to improve, people to hire, and constituents (parents, students, and taxpayers) to satisfy.

Yet time is short; there's never enough. So why should that precious commodity be spent communicating over process rather than just doing important educational tasks? Because good communication and collaboration make for an aligned organization, which is far more effective and efficient than an unaligned one.

Border issues—those issues that fall between roles—aren't always clear. But communication at the front end to clarify roles and process will save time and eliminate confusion later. The old adage that a good process will lead to a good result holds particularly true in an aligned school system.

Communicating Within the Board

Good communication and collaboration are as essential *within* the board as they are between the board and other roles. Board members must conduct business openly and as a group before the public; as a result, the natural flow of communication among individual members is restricted. In most states, individual board members have no legal authority to independently represent or act on behalf of the school district. Consequently, they must direct their individual inclinations away from direct and independent action and toward a group decision-making process. Because school boards by law make decisions by consensus or majority vote, they're more representative in their outcomes. The tradeoff is that arriving at decisions takes more time, so communication and collaboration are essential to addressing the school organization's strategic needs in an efficient manner. The board has two choices in organizing itself to discuss issues and accomplish its work: It can either function as a board of the whole or form committees. Each option has its pros and cons.

The *board-of-the-whole* approach allows all members to receive information relevant to their agenda at the same time and in the same way, and to have equal say in all board decisions. It's also easier for administration to prepare for one group rather than for multiple groups. But time constraints limit the issues and needs that a board of the whole can consider, much less consider in depth. Because the board doesn't delegate issues to subgroups, it must deal with everything that comes before it; that usually takes more time than boards have.

Many boards respond to this time crunch by forming *committees*. This option encourages some board members to become specialists in certain areas and ultimately creates more time to address issues. But board committees only truly save time if, at whole-board meetings, their members resist the urge to replay committee meetings to "catch up" the rest of that board. If they yield to that urge, committees consume more whole-board time than the board intended to save by forming the committee in the first place.

Another disadvantage is that committee members will have more information on some topics than the board as a whole. To be efficient, the board will normally follow the committees' lead in considering and deciding upon issues that come before the board, which puts a high premium on trust in committee members' judgment. If that trust is lacking, committees will drain time. A third disadvantage is that with increased individual board expertise comes an increased temptation to micromanage by dividing into tactical and operational decisions. When multiple board committees all succumb to this temptation, board micromanagement can run rampant.

Finally, board committees require considerable administrative and other staff time to prepare for and to organize meetings, something popularly referred to as "feeding the beast." The more "beasts" that require feeding, the less time tactical staff members have to carry out their regular work. The board must therefore decide how much time administrative staff can devote to board support at the expense of organizational duties.

Table 3-1 summarizes the advantages and disadvantages of each approach.

Table 3-1: Board of the Whole vs. Board Committees

Board of the Whole	Board Committees
Allows all members to receive information at the same time and in the same way, and to have an equal say in all board decisions	Encourages some board members to specialize in certain areas on behalf of the full board, creating more total time to address issues
Is easier for administration, as materials are prepared for one body rather than for multiple groups	Saves time if, at regular board meetings, members resist the urge to replay committee discussions to "catch up" the rest of the board
Limits time that the board can devote to issues and needs, particularly in depth	Requires board members to trust in committees because nonmembers don't have the same background and information on issues
Forces the entire board to deal with every issue	Can increase the likelihood of board micromanagement

Your board will determine which structure to adopt according to the manner in which you and other members wish to communicate and collaborate with each other in making decisions. If your board wants everyone to be equally informed on every issue, it will probably choose the board-of-the-whole approach. If your board wants its members to develop areas of specialty so that they acquire a deeper understanding of certain issues, it will opt for the committees approach. Either option is workable. It is critical to identify the particular collaboration and communication styles favored by the individuals on your current board. You will have to remake this choice each time board membership changes.

Communicating Across System Roles

To accomplish its own work as part of the district whole and to work with each other, each role—the board, administration, and teachers—requires collaborative structures and communication processes (see appendix, *Communication Structures and Processes*, page 132), which take time and resources to maintain. At their best, these structures and processes are tied to scheduled meetings and activities that support organizational goals.

Just as the board uses communication processes and collaborative structures, so do administration and teachers. (Organizational flow charts usually indicate these structures.) For example, administrative committees meet regularly so that tactical planning and implementation can be coordinated and standardized across the school organization. At the individual school, grade-level or departmental teacher-teams co-ordinate operational activities such as instructional unit plans or grading processes. In data-driven schools, teachers also meet regularly to share and analyze objective data on student performance to improve their instruction. (See appendix, *Collaborative Leadership Structures,* p. 133.) Although board members aren't directly involved in these structures and processes, they should still understand that additional time and resources are required to sustain them.

It's tempting to set up too many structures and processes. For example, in many school organizations, multiple structures deal with employee issues. This is a sign of two things. First, if many employee issues are raised on a regular basis, employee relationships with administration—and by extension with the board—aren't very good. In this case, the *relationship* needs more attention than the issues, which are largely byproducts of the poor relationship. Our "prescription"? Treat the "disease" (the overall relationship), not the "symptoms" (individual incidents).

Second, consider how many structures are necessary to deal with relationship issues. If the administration deals effectively with such issues, the answer is *one.* Any more will just create redundancies and interfere with the administration's work. Multiple structures that purport to do the same thing are misaligned and competitive, and draw time and resources away from meeting the organization's goals.

> Chances are, the more structures and processes dedicated to staff relationship issues, the worse the staff relationships.

How should the board respond to employee discontent? Unless the board itself is the issue, its role remains strategic. The board shouldn't engage in the tactical and operational discussions taking place among administration and staff; rather, it should charge administration to assess the extent to which staff is committed to the school organization's goals and why. This information will reveal any significant employee issues; the board's focus should remain on organizational goals rather than isolated instances of employee discontent.

The board must also monitor the temptation to create structures and processes to address needs or issues that aren't central to the school district. These needs and issues tend to emerge in a random way, one by one; it's unclear at first blush how they are connected or part of a larger theme. As the board more clearly sets and articulates its organizational goals, these themes become easier to identify, and isolated issues become understood and resolved within those themes.

> Communication processes and collaborative structures must service the goals of the organization, because each process and structure demands organizational time, resources, and personnel.

Align Communications

A board's most important task is to drive the school organization toward becoming an aligned school system. This commitment can be easily lost among the choppy sea of details and nonstrategic issues many boards assume they have to consider.

Serving on a board is much like trying to instill good character in a child: No single lesson or action results in the development of character. Character is built only through years of making choices between what's easy and what's right.

Systematic structures and processes are the organizational equivalents of a parent's unyielding commitment to the "right" choices. They become the compass by which a board can stay focused on true north: an aligned and continuously improving school system.

Yet aligning communication and collaboration across roles isn't easy. For example, for the board, the implementation of a new reading series may seem to involve only the time difference between its approval of the series and its initial use at the start of the following school year. The board may think, "We made our decision. Now we can go on to something else, because this will be in place in the fall."

For administrators, implementation means acquiring and distributing the materials, arranging for staff development on how to use them, and following up to make sure the implementation really occurs as planned. The administration may think, "Most of our work is now in front of us. We have a lot of organizing and coordinating to do, but by the time school starts, we should have most of this under control, provided we have a good follow-up plan in place."

For teachers, implementation means trying to get up to speed quickly on the new series, integrating it into existing lesson plans, and learning its details and nuances over the next year before they really are comfortable with using it in daily instruction. Teachers might think, "I hope we get some training on this before school starts. I hope I won't have to throw out all my old lesson plans, because I don't know where I'll find the time to replace them. It'll be at least a year before I feel comfortable using this series!"

Create Bridge Structures

This example demonstrates how the "languages" of strategic, tactical, and operational roles differ. The same "message" is read from completely different perspectives on what needs to be done and the time needed to do it—and elicits very different emotional responses. Accordingly, the bridge structures and processes discussed in chapter 2 are necessary to help "translate" messages across roles. Bridge structures span neighboring roles: parents and community members to board, board to administration, and administration to teachers. Rarely do such structures "jump" roles from, say, board to teachers. Typical bridge structures include advisory committees, strategic planning councils, and leadership teams that involve both parents and staff.

Advisory committees craft recommendations for board consideration, but don't have decision-making authority. In theory, the board can reject their recommendations. But in reality, the longer an advisory committee is functional, and the more representative of stakeholders it is, the more difficult it will be for a board to ignore those recommendations. When it does so, the board has in effect created a powerful opposition group to what the board is proposing, which may result, for example, in the defeat of a referendum that the board wants.

Advisory committees provide a more short-term way to gather information about community values and beliefs. These committees typically are a mix of staff, parents, and other citizens who meet on specific areas of concern, such as finances and facilities, instruction and curriculum, and communications.

We have two caveats about advisory committees:

1. As noted earlier, advisory committees can sometimes compete with district goals, rather than support them.

2. The "feed-the-beast" phenomenon concerning board committees applies equally to advisory groups; they consume a lot of administrative staff time and rob administrators of time to pursue tactical initiatives. Be aware upfront of this time tradeoff.

> A board can't carry out its strategic goals without communicative and collaborative assistance from its administrative staff, nor can the administration carry out aligned initiatives without the board's strategic guidance.

The reality is that no board can successfully interface with any constituent group without staff support, particularly by administrators. This puts high demands upon the development of efficient communication and collaboration processes and structures. Every aligned school system needs this kind of partnership, and no unaligned system of schools can improve its functioning without it. We'll discuss advisory committees in more depth later in this chapter.

A *strategic planning council* develops a long-term vision for the school organization. The board then crafts its own strategic direction, expressed as school organization goals, based on that vision. The more representative the strategic planning council is, the more the public will believe the resulting vision is rooted in the community's culture and beliefs.

A *district leadership team* contains representatives of all stakeholder groups—board members, administrators, certified and uncertified staff, parents, other community members, and sometimes students. The team usually has four purposes:

1. To listen to and learn from stakeholders in terms of their needs and requirements

2. To translate those needs and requirements into strategic plan recommendations

3. To assist in the tactical and operational monitoring of the school organization's goals

4. To report the results of this monitoring to the board

Each member usually is connected to a larger constituent group; for example, a parent is linked to the PTA or other parent organization. School representatives also serve on the school leadership team, which is similar to the district leadership team but operates on the school level. Team members are thus well-positioned to facilitate two-way communication with their constituent groups.

Most school organizations also create bridge structures among administration, teachers, and the teachers union. For example, on an instruction-curriculum committee, administrators and teachers meet to balance tactical plans and operational realities. Regular meetings between administrators and representatives of the teachers union to discuss contractual issues form another bridge. (Administration is well advised to view the union as a partner in making tactical and operational decisions, particularly because union leaders usually have more credibility with teachers than do either administrators or board members.) These three groups must be able to communicate in a safe, nonthreatening way so that their work can become deeply collaborative. This occurs when individuals throughout the system can reflect on and learn from their mistakes through open exchanges.

Unfortunately, in many school districts, various stakeholder groups have trouble listening to one another and thereby shut themselves off from the system's "bottom-up data"—information that flows from a role level below the decision-making one. Two examples:

1. Administrators that are considering an implementation schedule may ignore teacher concerns about time commitments teachers have already made.

2. A board that's considering a new initiative might ignore administrative concerns that the new initiative will eliminate an ongoing initiative that's halfway to full implementation.

Without shared information, stakeholders won't understand the obstacles they must collaboratively address to improve the system. The system must build trust between stakeholder groups so that accurate, understandable information can flow up and down the system's hierarchy. Bridge structures help everyone learn about the process of change and how different stakeholders perceive changes. When everyone understands what is important and expected, tremendous organizational growth can occur.

Understand Strategic, Tactical, and Operational Languages

The board's challenge is to make certain that it communicates those expectations in user-friendly language that's suited to each role. As Studer (2003) points out, "Communicating at all levels is critical, and we can improve how we cascade information throughout the organization, the breadth and depth of information we provide, and how we connect the dots on our actions for all stakeholders" (p. 73).

Communication is essential because people in different roles will construe the same action differently. For example, administrators (tactical staff) can misinterpret the board's goal to create more curricular rigor as an attempt to micromanage, while teachers (operational staff) may view it as just one more new thing on their plates. Parents, meanwhile, may see the board's strategic charge as taking time and resources away from things that they believe are more important.

These different perspectives can result in misinterpretations of and resistance to legitimate strategic goals, even when personality or other individual differences aren't issues. The board in particular should understand two things about such misinterpretation. First, they're more likely to result from role-based differences of perception than from different attitudes or agendas; therefore, when something goes wrong or resistance occurs, the board should look to communications processes before looking to individuals.

Second, the further another role is from the strategic role, the more likely it is that the board's strategic intent will be misinterpreted. For example, teachers are more likely to misinterpret the board call for more curricular rigor than are administrators. Similarly, non-parent community members likely will be more opposed to spending money for reduced class sizes than parents because the former are further from the direct effects of such changes.

The board needs to assure administration that it doesn't have to abandon other initiatives to which it is already committed, especially if these initiatives can also improve overall curricular rigor. What matters is that the board's goal becomes an administrative priority. However, the board should allow administration to achieve closure on prior commitments, particularly those that teachers have also embraced. The strategic and tactical roles, then, have to communicate continuously to ensure that they address both roles' needs and commitments, not just the board's strategic desires alone.

Likewise, teachers need to discuss with administrators, who are proxies for the board's intent, how both operational and tactical staff will shift time and resources to address the board's charge. Yet the importance of the board's strategic priority might erode before it reaches the operational level. To a teacher who feels that there's already not enough time available to do what he believes is expected of him, the board's charge might simply appear to be just one more burden to bear. So the operational role's question, "How many things do I have to do in my teaching and planning day?" has to be addressed to obtain teachers' buy-in to the board's new strategic charge.

Understand Operational Staff Fears

Good intentions aren't enough; what matters is how you communicate intentions across roles. In communicating with staff, you should keep three things in mind:

1. Staff members often read "hidden meanings" into comments and body language.

2. Staff members often believe the board has unlimited power and isn't afraid to use it.

3. Staff members usually assume that any board-initiated change will likely not be good for staff and that boards show a lack of concern for their needs.

For all these reasons, staff may fear board actions, even if such fear is unwarranted. Good board communication across roles can help allay such fears.

Hidden Meanings

Some staff members spend a lot of time analyzing each motion and word made at board meetings. They might read subtle implications into the board member's tone of voice, shift of position in a chair, or use of particular words (usually made spontaneously by the board member, who is oblivious to the implications being drawn). If nothing else, the board doesn't have enough time to be that subtle, even if it needed to be, which it doesn't.

Why do some staff members read so much into so little? Because they're usually trying to understand the board's strategic decisions from tactical and operational perspectives. They lack a strategic-tactical or tactical-operational bridge to help translate strategic priorities into their language (at least until the superintendent or principal can serve that bridge function). In addition, the board's strategic oversight role is largely a mystery to staff (with the exception of the superintendent and other administrators who regularly work closely with board members). After all, staff members only see the board in action at its public meetings, but miss the bulk of the preparatory study, communication, and other work that provide context to the board's decisions.

Context is everything when it comes to understanding. If people lack contextual understandings of why decisions are made, they'll create their own explanations. These incorrect contextual explanations often will be believed.

Unlimited Power

The widespread staff perception that the board's power is unfettered occurs because strategic decisions can supersede tactical or operational decisions. But this perception differs sharply from that of board members themselves, who know that their power is restricted in many ways. These include political limitations; restrictions on intra-board communications; open-meeting laws; state, federal, and other legal requirements; the difficulty in making organizational change really happen; and staff, parent, and community pushback.

Political limitations can include obligations new board members feel they must address due to their election and levels of community support, pressures they may receive from friends and neighbors, or community members' demands that board members can neither comfortably support nor politically ignore. Intra-board communications are generally restricted in various ways by sunshine laws and open-meetings acts in most states, and state and federal statutes and case law dictate many board decisions.

Organizational change itself is cumbersome, time-consuming, and difficult. A typical school district is a multileveled organization representing many constituent positions and views. In addition, the local tax-supported nature of most school districts makes every community member feel that he or she should have a voice in school decisions. For these reasons, any proposed change will simultaneously foster support among some and opposition among others, when the board's goal is overall consensus and community satisfaction.

Lack of Concern for Staff Needs

Staff members sometimes believe that the board isn't looking out for its best interests. For teachers, this feeling stems in part from board involvement in contract negotiations, which often are somewhat adversarial (though these negotiations also are usually the one time when some teachers work closely with board members). Such an adversarial setting is not conducive to building strong, positive relationships. Another "bump in the road" occurs when teachers are terminated either for cause or by a reduction-in-force resolution. Although the board might not be involved in such decisions, they might contribute to teachers feeling that the board isn't looking out for their best interests.

Administrators feel the issue of a board not looking out for staff's best interests more deeply and personally. Administration, starting with the superintendent, has the most direct contact and the closest working relationship with the board of any staff and is typically the most knowledgeable of all staff groups on board decisions. Yet administration is the first place that most boards look to when something goes wrong and they want to determine who's responsible. And it's also the first place boards seek cost savings, particularly regarding decisions around salaries and benefits.

Administrators also know that the board may condense what they do over the course of a school year to how administrators perform during the spring, when their evaluations typically take place. And in any school district, spring is when things are most likely to go wrong. Everyone is weary by the end of a typical school year—teachers, administrators, students, parents, and board members alike. Spring is when staff members are terminated; parents are tired of waiting for changes they have advocated for throughout the year; contract negotiations are in full swing; students smell the onset of summer and act accordingly; and projected budget shortfalls dramatically take center stage. It's a season of high anxiety in school circles, the worst time and circumstances for reasoned, thoughtful, and long-term evaluations of administrators to take place.

Respond to Staff Concerns

The bottom line: There are many reasons why the board can make staff feel insecure, even when that's not the board's intention. An astute board recognizes this reality and tries to counteract it by:

- Communicating publicly and privately its confidence in staff

- Setting clear and attainable board goals so that staff doesn't have to guess what the strategic priorities are

- Resisting the temptation to tactically micromanage

- Establishing evaluation procedures that are tied to board goals and that look at how well the administrator has functioned throughout the entire school year, rather than just during the spring

- Collaborating with staff to set timelines for implementing school district goals

All this cross-role communication is essential to avoid creating the adversarial "us versus them" culture in which communication among the strategic, tactical, and operational roles is neither timely nor effective. One of the most important indicators of a high-performing organization is the ability of all stakeholder groups to trust one another and to "pull in the same direction." Effective communication across roles is a key factor in ensuring that kind of teamwork.

When board members and staff successfully communicate across roles, strategic goals and measures take on new, more powerful significance because they are aligned with tactical and operational behaviors and actions. The board's strategic goals need to be translated into tactical language for staff leaders—superintendent, other administrators, teacher team leaders, union leadership—so they can clearly understand how these goals will affect their work and the expectations that the board has set for them. As the tactical data that administrators need is different from the kind of data the board requires, so do strategic goals need to be translated into the distinctive languages of teachers and other staff, families, and students. This is illustrated in Table 3-2 (page 46), which is adapted from the work of Rick Stiggins (2006). (For more on Stiggins' approach, see appendix, *Rick Stiggins' EDGE Analysis of Assessment System Users and Uses,* page 134.)

Stiggins (2006) shows how different kinds of questions for each role are aligned to address the same strategic targets. This alignment strengthens strategic goals and measures, and allows people at all levels to focus on the same overriding strategic targets.

How does communication across roles actually take place? One strategy is quarterly or three-times-a-year *employee forums or staff meetings* moderated by district or school leaders. Studer (2003) suggests that such events offer an opportunity to communicate a consistent message to all employees and to learn about and celebrate workplace successes. The meeting agenda is linked to the school district's strategic goals and measures, is organized around a theme that supports the school district's mission, and offers an opportunity for teamwork. Such events provide a forum for the school district to communicate key words or concepts that can help recommit staff to the school district's goals. Examples include celebrating positive changes in organizational performance results or acknowledging performance that exceeds expectations. These events also transmit consistent organizational messages and allow staff members to clarify their understanding of those messages and to ask specific questions about their responsibilities.

A second strategy involves the use of a *communication board*—a display of written communication that lays out key words and concepts and their relationships to the school's strategic goals. Communication boards help employees at all levels to connect their work to the school district's goals and performance results. (See the appendix, *Classroom Communication Boards*, page 136, for examples.)

Studer (2003) notes that a communication board ensures all employees have access to key information about strategic goals. Communication boards can help consistently get across the school district's goals at the program, school, team, department, or classroom level, so that every individual knows how he or she contributes toward achieving the organization's goals. The specific information found on a communication board varies at each level of the organization, while the strategic goal stays constant. The chart in Table 3-3 takes Studer's concept and applies it to a public education setting.

Table 3-2: Questions, Data, and Implications Across Roles

	Important Question to Be Answered	Information Needed to Answer the Question	Implications for the System
Strategic	What standards are to be met?	Learning targets in the form of achievement standards organized by grade and subject	Assessments must accurately reflect these standards.
Tactical	What standards are students expected to master by subject across our range of grade levels and classrooms?	Learning targets in the form of achievement standards organized by grade and subject as they unfold within and across grade levels	Assessments must accurately reflect these standards and their associated classroom learning targets.
Operational	What are my students supposed to learn? What is my child supposed to learn? What am I to learn?	Standards de-constructed into classroom targets leading, over time, to each standard; district curriculum maps of learning progression Learning targets in family-friendly and student-friendly language provided from the beginning of learning	All assessments must reflect these tactical targets; it must be clear which target any assessment reflects. Accurate assessments must reflect the learning targets students are given.

Source: Stiggins (2006)

Boards can't achieve their strategic goals without the active support of staff; thus, it's in the board's strategic interest to proactively cultivate that support. This process increases greatly the likelihood of the board's goals actually being attained throughout the school district. When it fails to cultivate staff, the board allows common role-based fears to color staff's perceptions of the board and its intent. The result is that school district change will be slowed at best and halted at worst.

Studer (2003) suggests three interactive communication strategies for focusing on positive outcomes:

1. Celebrate wins.

2. Manage for outcomes.

3. Share examples of employees who are making a difference. (p. 142)

Table 3-3: Example of a Strategic Communication Board

Student Achievement	Learning Environment	Satisfaction Surveys	Quality of Staff	Finance
State assessment results	Attendance rates	Results of student satisfaction survey	Highly qualified staff	State financial rating
Norm-referenced achievement test	Organization health survey	Results of parent satisfaction survey	Percentage of staff who have masters degrees or are in a continuing education program	Debt
Norm-referenced test to measure student academic growth	Class size	Results of community satisfaction survey	Competitive salary comparisons	Audit findings
Common assessment aligned to district grade-level or subject-level essential benchmarks	Discipline—suspensions, expulsions, and referrals	Results of staff satisfaction survey	Staff attendance record	Cash reserves
Graduation rate	Facility utilization		Number of grievances	Budget to actual
Number of students in high school Advanced Placement courses	Facility needs assessment		Staff retention data	Balance in all operating funds
Results compared to benchmark districts	State report card student data compared to benchmark districts		State report card data compared to benchmark districts	Financial data, such as revenues and expenditures per pupil, compared to benchmark districts
Results compared to highest performing districts	State report card student data compared to highest performing districts		State report card staff data compared to highest performing districts	Financial data compared to highest performing districts

Celebrate Wins

As a board, ask yourself, "What 'wins' have we achieved since we last met, and how are we communicating them throughout the system?" You might wonder whether, given the board's strategic role, it shouldn't maintain its strategic distance from celebrations. Won't the proximity of board members to employees carry the risk of board micromanaging? In this case, absolutely not. By stressing positive results, the board can lessen that distance between itself and everyone else. And board members, in coordination with the superintendent, are the ideal people to organize celebratory talks and events. Such events are a great way for board members to "put a human face" on the board while also promoting a message of organizational excellence and encouraging all employees to strive for what some of their best colleagues have already achieved.

Manage for Outcomes

Provide opportunities for feedback about employee satisfaction. Do so with a personal touch by including essential questions that respond to employee needs. You might start with an "ice-breaking" question to establish a personal connection, such as "How was your trip in today?" or "Do you have a vacation planned any time soon?" These should be followed by such queries as:

- "Tell me what is working well today."
- "Are there any of your coworkers who I should be recognizing?"
- "Is there anything you feel we can do better?"
- "Do you have the right tools and equipment to do your job?"

Share Examples of Employees Who Are Making a Difference

Use specific examples of employees who have performed outstanding work, initiated a successful change or innovation, or helped coworkers achieve success. The power of this action isn't in the recognition of a particular employee, although that can also result in employee appreciation, but in the specificity of the example used to justify the recognition. The more clear and specific the example, the more likely other employees will successfully be able to replicate it in their own work. This also has the added advantage of showing through example the expectations of management in a positive and supportive way.

Concerning management leaders, Larry Bossidy and Ram Charan (2002) advise:

> You need robust dialogue to surface the realities of an organization. You need accountability for results—discussed openly and agreed to by those responsible—to get things done and celebrate success. You need follow-through to ensure the plans are on track. Dialogue and communication is the core of culture and the basis unit of work. How people talk to each other absolutely determines how well the organization will function. Is the dialogue stilted, politicized, fragmented, and butt-covering? Or is it candid and reality-based, raising the right questions, debating them, and finding realistic solutions? If it's the former—as it is in all too many companies—reality will

never come to the surface. If it is to be the latter, the leader has to be on the playing field with his management team, practicing it consistently and forcefully. (p. 23)

Bossidy and Charan's observation pertains not only to management leaders, but also to school board members. In their interactions with the superintendent and other senior tactical administrative staff, boards must strike a balance between candid, reality-based dialogue and respectful, team-based problem-solving. Achieving this balance is the most effective way to align board and staff efforts at the strategic and tactical levels; it assumes a *partnership of purpose* among the board, the superintendent, and its senior administrators. This partnership of purpose allows the school district's leadership to achieve great things. When it's missing, no amount of effort or forceful demands from any level will move the school district forward.

Administering satisfaction surveys and using the results in candid discussions around organizational goals and issues can identify staff strengths and weaknesses, as well as the feelings of the community base—especially when such surveys are aligned to board goals and initiatives, both at the present and over time. The combination of satisfaction survey data and more objective outcomes data gives the board powerful guidance on how to move forward in meeting its strategic goals and initiatives.

Communicating With Constituents

The board typically interfaces with five constituent groups:

1. Administration
2. Staff
3. Students
4. Parents
5. Community members

Administration

The board requires information from administrators on how board goals are being carried out through tactics. This information can come in the form of written reports or presentations to the whole board or to board committees. At board meetings, and particularly at committee meetings, board members and administration should communicate on specific topics they have defined in advance on a formal meeting agenda.

Staff

The board should have limited direct contact with school staff. For example, it would be inappropriate for a board member to sit in on a meeting between a principal and his or her staff. Board members shouldn't become involved in discussions on areas where their strategic role leaves them ill-prepared to come to sound conclusions about tactics or operations. Your limited time is much better spent setting strategic charges and understanding the impact of tactics in actualizing these charges.

There are a few exceptions. In collective bargaining, board members typically sit at the negotiating table and directly interact with a representative of the teachers union. This is because resources are at stake—clearly a board responsibility. Another exception occurs when teachers or other operational staff members come to a board meeting to present children or to demonstrate a teaching program or instructional approach. Though the board might receive some useful information, the meeting's essential purpose is public relations—to promote pride in the quality of teaching found within the school organization.

A third exception concerns shared leadership interactions, such as leadership teams or strategic planning committees that have teacher representatives. In these cases, the intent is to help each role understand the perspectives of the other two through direct representation and to come to a big-picture, visionary conclusion. Such meetings also provide contextual background for board members to become better informed about tactical and operational realities around specific educational initiatives before they formulate strategic charges (the first step in the decision-making cycle discussed in chapter 2). These meetings provide stakeholders a voice into charges that the board has made or will make in the future.

A final exception isn't a true exception, since it concerns a personal interaction and not a formal board interaction. Most board members are also parents who interact with their children's teachers, as almost all parents do. The trick isn't to wear your board hat on those occasions, which is particularly hard because the teacher will see you first as a board member and only second as a parent. If you find yourself in this situation, you'll likely be unable to convince the teacher to do otherwise, no matter what you do or say. Teachers are usually intimidated by board members, regardless of an individual board member's personality.

Students

The closest board members usually get to students is when students attend a board meeting to make a presentation about an exceptional achievement or event—a pure public relations moment.

Ironically, as a parent, you might have a very personal experience with the school through your own children, but as a board member, your involvement with children is anything but personal. At board meetings, children are often considered more as data points on test score summaries and enrollment lists than as living, breathing people. Unfortunately, when the board-student encounter does become more personal, it usually occurs in a closed-session board review of a disciplinary matter, such as a student suspension or expulsion.

Parents

This can be the trickiest area for board communications. Parents feel a natural alliance with the board member, whom they view as "one of us." The advantage of this perspective is that a new board member usually has an initial reservoir of parent trust and confidence. (An exception may occur after a bitterly partisan board election.) However, one disadvantage is that parents might assume that the new board member will look out for *their* children's best interests, just as the new board member will for his or her own children. But remember that the board member is responsible for *all* the school district's children, not just some.

A second disadvantage is that many parents assume that the board member will view school issues through the same lens they do: focusing on the classroom, an individual child, specific teachers, and a single principal. Parents might want the board member to focus on specific instructional and curricular issues that affect their children—for example, how much homework teachers assign, whether weekly spelling tests are given, what kinds of grades a child receives, or how teachers and principals discipline children. These matters are all operational and so are naturally in conflict with the board member's strategic perspective. Board members are friends and neighbors to many parents. But if you act on behalf of a parent as a friend or neighbor rather than as a board member, you immediately compromise your objectivity.

Fortunately, board policies can assist you in this kind of situation—if you use them. These policies typically include a process for addressing complaints, beginning at the level that's closest to the incident that generated the complaint. As a board member, you're the furthest removed from the incident, so the policy probably recommends that you not deal directly with the complaint, but rather pass it on to someone closer to the incident.

This is an example where the collaborative structure and the communicative process are not always automatically aligned. A board member rarely can say to a friend or a neighbor, "Please go see the teacher. I don't involve myself at this level." But even if you did involve yourself, you couldn't react in a responsible manner because you would only know one side of the story, and you wouldn't have any individual authority by which to offer a solution.

What can you do in that situation? Listen. As a caring and sympathetic listener, you can also offer to bring the complaint to the superintendent's attention; he or she will see to it that the complaint is handled by the right person. In this way, you can be responsive as a friend or a neighbor, while staying within your strategic role as a board member. Resist the urge to use your board position to please your friends or your neighbors; don't put a momentary desire to be liked before your strategic responsibilities. Rather, promise to contact the superintendent and have him or her investigate the situation; you can promise to contact the parent with the results of the investigation. Through this process, the parent should feel a sense of closure to the issue, while you've acted in a way appropriate to your role.

In communicating with constituents, a board member must be careful not to respond with solutions to tactical or operational issues. Even if the request seems simple and the response appears obvious or something that staff would "automatically" do, you should respond as a board member. Parents may request action, but you should only offer communication.

For example, say that a parent, after providing a very passionate and convincing argument that a teacher unfairly singled out her child for harder work, asks you to address why her child wasn't given the same assignment as her neighbor's child. Do you:

A. Agree with the parent and promise to correct the problem?

B. Call the teacher involved and tell him to correct the problem?

C. Contact the principal and direct her to correct the problem?

D. Speak to the superintendent and ask him to investigate the matter to see if there really is an issue at all?

The answer is D. If the parent is correct and the assignment was in fact unfair, the superintendent will contact the proper people to correct the situation. If the parent isn't correct—if, for example, her child's assignment was longer because the student hadn't completed a previous assignment, but had neglected to tell the parents about that important detail—then the matter can stop with the superintendent. He or she won't needlessly have to upset a principal or teacher for something that isn't true. The other choices are inappropriate because a board member, in choosing any of them, would be assuming a tactical or operational role and bypassing the superintendent, who has the legal responsibility to oversee staff activities.

By effectively addressing your strategic responsibilities, you'll likely please most parents, but displease those whose operational issues you haven't responded to. From the disappointed parent's perspective, you've crossed over to "the dark side" because you've apparently abandoned your original "loyalty" as "one of us." Some parents might even believe that you've been "taken over" by the school district (usually the superintendent, to whom parents ascribe more authority than he or she ever really has).

Being able to know the parents' orientation will allow you to see an individual parent's complaint in proper perspective. In a well-run school district, parents' issues are addressed at other levels, making your direct involvement unnecessary. Don't become directly involved in an operational issue when asked, but instead listen empathically and refer the parental question or complaint to the superintendent. Your ability to empathically listen and appropriately refer, *without* directly acting yourself, means that you're properly bridging your strategic role with the parent's operational concerns.

Community Members

By law, the board must carry out the school district's business in public before an audience of interested citizens. It meets primarily to conduct business that can't be conducted by anyone else, as opposed to meeting to interact with community members; that's only a secondary purpose for board meetings.

On the other hand, the public sees a board meeting as its one access point to influence decisions made on behalf of the school district. To community members, the opportunity to interact with the board is fundamental to why it must meet in public. And the more passionately an audience member holds a point of view, the more important it is that he or she has the opportunity to address the board. It's even more important that the board acknowledges and accepts that point of view.

These different perspectives put the board and its audience at odds over the meeting's purpose. Most state laws recognize the competing purposes by requiring the board to allow the public to comment on board decisions. For its part, the public can voice opinions but can't interfere with the board's ability to carry out its business.

While the board ultimately holds final decision-making authority, how it publicly conducts its business is as important as what decisions it ultimately makes. If the board realizes that there are reasons why it sits apart from the audience, it can lessen the effects of that separation by understanding three things about the way it communicates with the public.

First, a public board meeting is not the same as a public forum; a public board meeting is not designed for a debate of issues between the board and the audience, nor is it the place for spontaneous discussion with community members. Again, the meeting's purpose is to make strategic decisions for the school district, and board members' time and energies must be devoted to this end.

> The board must realize that it inspires confidence with the public more through its behavior at public meetings than by its decisions.

The segment of each meeting devoted to audience comment is a time when the board either gains or loses good will from the public. The audience generally doesn't require a debate to be satisfied that its points were heard. Usually, it's sufficient that the board listen carefully and respectfully to remarks, thank the individual for commenting, and state how the school district will follow up.

Second, more than anything else, the public wants to believe that the board operates professionally, that it's *thoughtful, prudent, and responsible.* The board's only chance to demonstrate those qualities to the public is during its open meetings. If the board instead indicates that it's ill-prepared, impetuous, or confrontational, it will lose the public's confidence, no matter what decisions it makes. The board, therefore, can't engage in discussions for which it hasn't prepared without risking the professional image that it seeks to publicly promote. Professional behavior at public meetings is essential to garnering the public's respect and is an essential leadership ingredient in the development of an aligned school system.

Third, good board decisions aren't spontaneous but result from long hours of research, study, and discussion. Much of that process can be documented and shared with community members, usually through a packet of materials that is presented at board meetings or posted on school district websites.

While some community members might challenge the board's research, most will feel secure knowing that the board took a thoughtful approach to arriving at its decisions. It's impractical, if not impossible, for the board to document and share everything that went into its decision-making. Still, as it assesses the board's competence, the public will appreciate that the board's process was transparent.

Community members may also come to public board meetings to make requests or demands. Whether or not a board policy provides guidance for such instances, you should avoid entering into protracted public debate with individuals. In a public meeting, an audience member almost always appears as the underdog, no matter how inappropriate his or her statements might be. A public debate wins no audience sympathy for the board, forces it to make off-the-cuff decisions that haven't been re-searched or evaluated, and causes problematic tactical and operational ripple effects.

If you're in such an encounter, first restate the individual's comments so that the speaker is assured that you fully understand the issue from his or her perspective; then direct the superintendent to look into the situation, and promise to respond individually to the audience member at a later date. This projects a thoughtful ap-proach and shows community members that the board can't be coerced into quick decisions based upon public pressure.

Boards also need access to the community, and not just to raise new funds through tax referenda. Periodically, your board should check the community's "pulse" to see whether board goals are in alignment with community values and beliefs.

Eliciting Feedback

A good rule of thumb is: Don't ask about issues if you aren't willing to seriously consider changing policies, particularly when soliciting opinions from the public. The board interacts with administration, staff, parents, and others in the community at their respective constituent levels. The board has to understand the perspectives of each constituency on various topics and take into account how each perspective may differ or be in conflict with another. Typically, boards can gauge constituent feelings formally, through written surveys or town hall–like meetings, or informally, through discussion with constituents.

In collecting both formal and informal constituent information, the board should decide upfront what the purpose of such information will be. If the board wants formal polling information, it should either align the information to school district goals or generate data that allow the board to consider different goals. Don't launch into formal data gathering, which can be highly staff intensive, if there isn't first a strong correlation between the type of data collected and the existing or likely goals of the school district.

Formal polling will produce reliable data if the survey instruments are sound, which the board should require and staff that is trained in data gathering can collect, analyze, and explain. The board won't know whether anecdotal data are reliable, no matter how convincing the person who related it may have sounded. If anecdotal data don't match formal data on a particular topic, they shouldn't be considered reliable; formal data will need to be obtained to validate the anecdotal perspective (provided that the time staff spends collecting such data isn't too great).

A formal survey or other poll provides broad trend data that are reliable if the survey queries a representative sample of the constituent group. However, survey data are weak in terms of lacking individual detail. An anecdote has the opposite problem: While it contains an individual perspective, it isn't representative of a larger group. A third possibility, a town hall–like meeting, has fewer strengths, but fewer weaknesses; it's rich in anecdotal detail and likely representative of those who attend (assuming they feel comfortable speaking), though it might not be representative of the community as a whole (you can't assume that the attendees are a representative cross-sample). People who attend such meetings tend to cluster as subgroups rather than represent a cross-section of a constituent base.

> Anecdotal data may sound very convincing, but they don't have enough depth or breadth to replace good objective data. An anecdote that the board finds particularly compelling should serve as a call for the collection of formal data to validate or invalidate the perspective found in the anecdote. The board shouldn't make decisions based upon anecdotes alone.

The bottom line is that in developing its view on an issue, the board should obtain data from different sources before taking action. If those data match, the board has a legitimate perspective to consider; only then should it take action. If data from different sources don't match, the board probably lacks enough reliable information to seriously consider a different perspective.

An exception to the admonition about not asking about what you're unwilling to change concerns board-administration, particularly board-superintendent, interaction. The board needs to explore potential new strategic initiatives with someone in a different role. Tactical staff, particularly the superintendent, with his or her strategic-tactical bridge role, fits this purpose. Strategic-tactical discussions can vet new ideas from two different role perspectives. While doing so, individuals in both roles should keep the process confidential.

Why is confidentiality important? The board needs to consider ideas without necessarily acting on them. But the further a person sits from the board table, the less well he or she will understand this. To the mainly operational perspectives of a typical board audience (parents, other community members, and teachers), every board discussion can appear likely to lead to action, even when the board president specifically states that the board discussion is only exploratory and might not lead to any action. Given this, members of the public might mobilize in fierce opposition to what they believe is a pending proposal, thereby drawing the board into a defensive posture over something it never was going to seriously consider in the first place.

But because the board wants representative opinions from teachers, parents, and other community members to inform its deliberations, it will usually turn to survey instruments to obtain these opinions. The board that undertakes surveys will learn of stakeholders' views without risking the mobilization of opposition that a public debate might precipitate.

Survey for Satisfaction Data

Satisfaction data are derived from opinion surveys. These surveys don't measure outcomes, such as test scores, but rather perceptions about outcomes and activities. For example, they might measure parents' opinions about whether test scores are high enough. These perceptions are translated into data that indicate whether respondents feel positive or critical about specific aspects of a school district.

Even though satisfaction data are subjective, they are important because they reflect the degree of constituent support for the school district. It's crucial for a board that's continually trying to improve the district to assess such information. The board's commitment to districtwide change requires a firm base of community support. Satisfaction surveys provide objective data that align to measurements on a district performance scorecard in such categories as learning environment and customer service.

What makes a satisfaction survey well-constructed? Four things:

1. It is representative of the real opinions of those surveyed.

2. Its questions are aligned to strategic goals.

3. It is sensitive to stakeholder needs and employee satisfaction with the workplace.

4. It focuses on viable issues that the board is willing to change.

Representative of Real Opinions

The satisfaction survey should be designed to ensure that survey results will be valid or representative of respondents' real opinions. The board can inform those who create a satisfaction survey of the topics that it wants to see surveyed but shouldn't micromanage the survey's design. Rather, tactical staff members should develop (or purchase) the survey instrument because they have the necessary technical expertise to ensure that the survey will produce valid results.

Satisfaction surveys need to be focused on the views of particular constituent groups. For example, assume that your board is interested in the effectiveness of homework on how students learn. Along with directing tactical staff to research the effectiveness of homework, the board might request separate surveys to examine the different perspectives of teachers and parents. The questions for teachers might examine their perceptions regarding rates of homework completion and whether homework completion correlates to higher grades. The questions for parents might focus upon parental perceptions regarding the time it takes their children to complete the homework and whether parents feel it's challenging or merely "busy work." Because both surveys deal with homework, the board gets two different perspectives on this topic.

Aligned to Strategic Goals

Survey questions need to be aligned to strategic goals, though that isn't as easy as it might sound. That's because the surveys that schools purchase, often in order to meet quality standards for validity, seldom capture the school district's specific tactical and operational needs, much less its strategic goals. Consequently, the school district often has to develop its own surveys that are aligned to its own strategic goals. If these local surveys are not well-designed, their validity may be compromised.

When survey questions aren't aligned to strategic goals, the data generated can take the board and staff off task. For example, if a strategic goal is to introduce more curricular rigor for already high-achieving students, then surveying teachers about whether they think more rigor is needed will be counterproductive if a majority responds "no."

Sensitive to Stakeholder Needs and Employee Satisfaction

Survey questions also need to address stakeholder needs, particularly around employee satisfaction in the workplace. A school district can more effectively influence staff performance by focusing on how well the organization is meeting employees' needs. Marcus Buckingham and Curt Coffman (1999) report that the Gallup Organization spent over 25 years asking hundreds of questions to more than a million employees on every conceivable aspect of the workplace. Ultimately, they determined that the list of key questions could be reduced to 12, which follow. Although these questions don't capture everything you might want to know about employee satisfaction, they do reflect the core elements that are needed to attract, focus, and retain the most talented employees.

1. Do I know what is expected of me at work?

2. Do I have the materials and equipment I need to do my work right?

3. At work, do I have the opportunity to do what I do best every day?

4. In the last seven days, have I received recognition or praise for doing good work?

5. Does my supervisor or someone at work seem to care about me as a person?

6. Is there someone at work who encourages my development?

7. At work, do my opinions seem to count?

8. Do the mission and purpose of my company make me feel my job is important?

9. Are my co-workers committed to doing quality work?

10. Do I have a best friend at work?

11. In the last six months, has someone at work talked to me about my progress?

12. This last year, have I had opportunities at work to learn and grow? (p. 28)

A good staff satisfaction survey asks the essential questions that will determine whether respondents feel satisfied and productive about the services the organization provides. In addition, survey questions need to be aligned, meaning that students, families, and staff should reflect on similar issues. (See *Satisfaction Survey Alignment* in the appendix, page 137.)

Designing surveys to reflect school district alignment places at risk another board concern: the desirability of obtaining longitudinal data. Such data require asking the same question over multiple surveys so that you can compare answers over time. By using longitudinal data, the board continually monitors its support base. In this way, you can know whether your new initiatives have come at the expense of standard practices that have enjoyed community support. In the eyes of the community, no new initiative is likely to trump an existing one that enjoys popular support.

Yet by keeping surveys the same over time, the board might forfeit its ability to change a survey as needed to address its present goals and objectives. The board's study of an issue over the long term can directly conflict with its need for alignment in the short term. The board must decide which need is greater and then be specific about what it wants to know that's aligned to its goals, what it wants to understand over time, and how it will deal with survey results that aren't aligned. The board can then pass on its desires to tactical staff as guidelines for constructing the appropriate surveys.

Focused on Viable Issues for Change

The board shouldn't ask teacher, parent, and community groups about matters that it's unwilling to consider changing. These three groups tend to view anything they are asked to consider, especially through a survey or other formal process, as probable if they have supported the proposed change. In short, they assume that board decisions will follow overall sentiment indicated by the survey. Should the board feel and act otherwise, it risks teacher or community pushback, as reflected in such statements as "You wanted our opinion, we gave it to you, and now you're ignoring it" and "Why did you ask my opinion in the first place if you'd already made up your mind?" In effect, the board has mobilized informed opposition.

Share Survey Outcomes With Respondents

The results of satisfaction surveys are not just for the board alone. Though the information might be vital to the board's present and future considerations, the act of eliciting opinions from other groups involved those groups in the board's considerations to a significant degree. That involvement can't be ignored. Astute boards never undertake surveys without first planning on how to share the results with the respondents. Survey respondents were asked their opinion, have invested time and thought into answering questions, and want to know how their responses compare to those of others to bring closure to the experience. By publicly sharing the survey results, the board makes it more likely that subsequent surveys will garner equal or greater representative participation.

Report results quickly to everyone who took the survey. A deeper analysis of the results can take place after they're compiled and shared. Analysis shouldn't be an excuse for a failure to share results in a timely manner with respondents; the board and staff can undertake an in-depth analysis of the results after this has occurred. However, the board's feeling that it should carefully examine the data shouldn't serve as an excuse for not sharing it in a timely way, especially because the longer you take to share survey results, the less satisfied people are with the process. That general dissatisfaction tends to negatively impact responses to the results themselves.

After the results are shared, celebrations of student or staff achievement need to be planned and opportunities for improvement should be identified. Leaders who will share the results need to be trained how to clearly explain them to others. Once the data are reported to everyone, action plans— specific steps and timelines by which to address opportunities for improvement—should be developed, preferably with input from some of those surveyed. After being implemented, action plans should be studied to see if they have achieved the desired results, and accomplishments should again be reported to those surveyed. The survey cycle then begins anew as the most recent results are compared to previous results to measure how much improvement has occurred.

Use of Advisory Committees

Board advisory committees typically gather perspectives from a wide representation of constituent groups to address specific issues, using guidelines prescribed by the board. Here, the purpose is exploratory, or the opposite of most surveys, which are designed to confirm the direction the board has decided upon rather than to explore possible new options. While advisory committees provide the board recommendations from various perspectives, they shouldn't be seen as binding. The board is less likely to feel bound if it gives the advisory committee a clear charge from the outset (and periodic reminders after that) to explore existing policy options and to investigate possible alternatives, but not to determine board action.

For example, the board might ask an advisory committee to investigate the impediments to lowering class size (the maximum number of students allowed per classroom), given that current space constraints won't change, and to research how other schools in similar situations have dealt with this issue. This board charge is less restrictive than a charge that would have the committee recommend a specific numerical limit on class size and so would constrain the board's freedom of action. But no matter how carefully the board crafts a charge for an advisory committee, the committee might still make recommendations that it expects the board will follow or that are more restrictive for the board than the board would like.

The danger of forming an advisory committee is that the time and effort put forth by the committee's members must result in something useful and valuable to the board; otherwise, the members will feel that their time has been wasted and will feel resentment toward the board.

The classic example of such resentment can come about through the board's creation of a referendum exploratory committee—a well-meaning attempt to generate a representative base of community involvement that will then be in a position to lead the support for a later referendum drive. Often, as a result of their research, committee members are well-informed about and committed to the issue at hand, and will presumably "do the heavy lifting" in support of a referendum. But what if, in the middle of its research, an advisory committee recommends a particular approach or focus to the referendum that the board rejects? Now a well-informed organized group exists that opposes the board's position, and as a result, securing passage of the referendum becomes far more difficult, if not impossible.

Of course, in establishing the advisory committee, the board was trying to create a powerful support group, not powerful opposition. But it ignored the fundamental truth about advisory committees: Those involved in the research that occurs before a board decision usually have an increased desire to shape that decision.

Thus, before starting an advisory committee, the board must ask itself: "Will we be willing to follow the committee's recommendations, whatever they may be, or will we make the final decision entirely by ourselves?" If the board is unwilling to follow an advisory committee's advice or recommendations, it's better not to form the committee. This isn't as risky as it might sound, especially if the board has given no public indication that it might form a committee. In this case, the public might be much more likely to accept the board's sole decision (especially if the board is acting based upon good data from satisfaction surveys) than a decision that runs counter to an advisory committee recommendation.

One specific type of advisory group combines the district perspective of the district leadership team with the individual school perspectives of each of the school leadership teams. The result is rich detail from all three role perspectives—strategic, tactical, and operational—regarding common issues or objectives.

We've discussed the risks the board faces in forming an advisory committee, but there are some potential advantages that make taking such risks worthwhile. Such a committee can:

- Make board deliberations more inclusive and transparent and, as a result, generate staff and community support for its decisions.

- Provide the board very useful perspectives from important constituent groups, particularly when the committee's work aligns with the board's priorities.

- Conduct research that the board doesn't have time to do.

- Supply rich anecdotal information that lends weight to the more objective data being researched and considered.

- Promote positive bonding among its members, which will extend to the board, especially if some members and key staff members are members of the committee.

- Spread the word regarding positive experiences with the board and its school district to friends and neighbors of committee members.

All these characteristics of successful advisory groups represent huge political advantages for the board in terms of showing that the board is in touch with constituent needs and otherwise linked to the community.

Establishing Credibility

The more credible you are, the more likely it is that your message will be well-received. Credibility is not automatic with any position, and when you step outside your role, your credibility will be greatly diminished. Remember, each role has its own "language." Personal charisma and integrity can offset some of the communication obstacles, but most of us overestimate their power to mitigate problems. You need to acknowledge and accommodate other roles to enhance your credibility.

Generally, the further your role is from another, the less credibility you will have. Board members don't have as much credibility with teachers as other staff members do. On the other hand, board members generally have more credibility with parents and the community than staff members do, including teachers, because board members are parents and members of the community themselves.

This means that you have a direct, personal stake in the outcomes produced by the school organization. You aren't paid staff. You're unlikely to leave the community for a "better offer" somewhere else; you also pay taxes to support the school organization. You're a parent and a citizen, just like everyone else, but with a significant difference: You're in a public role. If you combine your credibility with the public with your understanding of all of the information on the school organization that the public doesn't have, you'll be in an enviable position to have a huge impact on your school district.

As a board member, you're in a unique and enviable position to truly and credibly determine the quality of learning your child and everyone's child will receive—to the extent you can successfully gauge and account for the needs of both community aspirations and organizational capacity.

Chapter Summary

- Being able to convincingly communicate board decisions is as important as, and often more important than, the decisions themselves.

- A board and its superintendent can't communicate too much.

- Boards should develop formal communication processes and collaborative structures to guide their work.

- Processes and structures take time, so they must be efficient to leave the bulk of time for organizational improvement.

Communicating Within the Board

- Boards can function as whole boards or organize themselves into committees; before choosing either option, the board should be aware of each option's advantages and drawbacks.

Communicating Across System Roles

- There can be too many structures and processes when they are redundant and unaligned.

- The more structures and processes are set up to deal with relationship issues, the more likely it is that the relationships themselves are poor.

- When a relationship is poor, treat the relationship itself, not the issues coming out of the relationship.

- The same message sounds different and has different meanings to different roles.

- People in different roles think about the same thing in different ways.

- Bridge structures and processes are required between board and community, board and administration, and administration and teachers.

- Typical bridge structures are advisory committees, strategic planning councils, and district leadership teams.

- Bridge structures help keep "bottom-up" data from being ignored.

- Role perspectives are naturally misunderstood by other roles.

- Boards need to communicate in language suited to the role or group they are addressing, not just in strategic language.

- It's natural for staff to fear potential board actions, even when that's not the board's intent.

- The board can counter this role-based fear through proactive planning and communication steps that assure staff that it has the board's confidence.

- Boards need to publicly celebrate "wins," especially for the sake of staff morale, to manage for outcomes, and to share examples of employees who are making a difference.

Communicating With Constituents

- The board communicates with five constituent groups: administrators, staff, students, parents, and community members.

- The board's communications with each group will be different from those with other groups.

- A board member's strategic role prevents him or her from responding to a parent's individual operational concerns.

- To bridge this gap, the board member must empathically listen to a parent and appropriately refer his or her issue to someone who can act on it, but should not act him- or herself.

- To the board, the purpose of its meeting is to conduct board business; to the audience, it's to directly interface with the board. Therefore, the two purposes are often in conflict.

- The board needs to satisfy an audience member's need for interaction but shouldn't engage in spontaneous debate with that individual and other audience members.

- The board needs to be professional at all times in order to keep the audience's trust and support.

- The board should share background information that supports board decisions with the audience at board meetings and the public through various communications tools.

Eliciting Feedback

- The board needs to take formal (objective and quantitative) and informal (subjective and anecdotal) surveys of various constituent groups.

- Anecdotal data are strong in detail but weak in representation, while survey data are the opposite.

- Boards shouldn't act on anecdotal data alone, but should match them to objective data to determine their validity.

- Boards can vet options in confidence with tactical staff, but shouldn't do so with other groups, except with board advisory committees.

- The board's strategic role is naturally at odds with a parent's operational concerns and a community member's desire, as a taxpayer, to influence board decisions.

- Satisfaction data identify overall levels of constituent support, give objective context to individual issues and complaints, and constitute objective information for a district performance scorecard.

- Boards need surveys that give clear and valid results, align to board goals, provide longitudinal data, and don't suggest options that the board is unwilling to consider.

- Participating in surveys encourages further involvement by respondents; as a result, boards should always share survey results with them.

- Board advisory committees mobilize their members, either in support of or in opposition to, the board, and thus are two-edged swords.

- Boards shouldn't form advisory committees if they're unwilling to seriously consider the committee's recommendations.

- Advisory committees usually make recommendations on tactics and should therefore report first to tacticians before making a final report to the board.

Establishing Credibility

- Effective communications depend upon your credibility, but that credibility is naturally weakened when you communicate across roles.

- Board members naturally have more credibility with parents and community members than with staff, particularly teachers.

4

10 Signals That Your Board Is in Trouble

Because the board has a 50,000-foot view, it won't see all of the tactical and, especially, the operational dynamics within the school district. The board's perspective is like looking at the outside of an anthill and trying to guess how many ants are underneath and what they're doing. But many boards feel they have 20/20 vision at every level of the school district because they see so clearly at their strategic level. But boards don't have 20/20 vision at all levels—no one in the school district does. And what the board can't see often affects, directly or indirectly, the successful implementation of its strategic vision and goals.

So what can you and other board members do with limited organizational vision? First, recognize that you don't need to see everything. Others have 20/20 vision at their levels for you, especially when all roles are working in an aligned, collaborative way. Conversely, the tactical and operational roles need your 20/20 strategic vision to provide the proper context to their work. When strategic, tactical, and operational roles are aligned, the entire school district has 20/20 vision.

Second, recognize that what you do see may not be enough to keep out of trouble. You'll have to become adept at "reading" some signals that your board isn't functioning well; we've identified 10 of them.

10 Signals That Your Board Is in Trouble

1. Engaging in partisan voting
2. Not supporting a majority board decision
3. Responding to community discontent without data or process
4. Conducting your own research
5. Applying expert advice literally without consulting staff
6. Ignoring the impact of culture on change
7. Not supporting district policies
8. Failing to foster a three-way partnership with the superintendent and union leaders
9. Hiring a superintendent on a split vote
10. Failing to personally detach from board decisions

#1 Engaging in Partisan Voting

When a board votes unanimously, the public often accuses the board of applying a "rubber stamp," as if unanimity automatically were a sign of weakness or an indication that administration is dictating board decisions. Yet for an aligned school board within an aligned school district, unanimous votes are common because each role is functioning efficiently within its own area of expertise and in collaboration with the other roles. In such a district, the board gives clear strategic charges, the administration crafts plans to carry them out, and teachers work hard to ensure that these plans will work in real classrooms with real children. There's a place for split boards, especially when the board is first developing its strategic charges. Board members might have honest disagreements about how to set the board goal or charge, which may result in a split vote. A split vote communicates to the public that a particular issue is complex and that there's no solution that meets all stakeholder needs.

Two factors determine whether a split vote is positive (it maintains board and school district alignment) or negative (it pulls the board out of alignment with the rest of the school district):

1. Why the split vote occurred

2. How the board acts after the vote

Neither concerns the content of what was approved.

Some split votes occur because board members honestly express differing perspectives; the split is *idea-based* and derives from the inherent representative nature of the board. An idea-based split vote shouldn't signal trouble to the board unless disagreements over the differing ideas can't eventually become resolved through further discussion that leads to consensus.

However, when a split vote isn't idea-based, consensus becomes far more difficult to achieve, because board members are engaging in partisan voting. *Partisan votes substitute emotional commitment for objective analysis.* A partisan vote is characterized by coalitions among some board members that have been formed expressly to oppose others—"I'm going to vote 'no' because you're going to vote 'yes.'"

This partisan approach is easy to spot because subgroups of board members almost always vote the same way, regardless of the issues brought forward. This contrasts with idea-based votes, in which board members shift their positions relative to other board members during each deliberation. The partisan approach is hard to change because personal coalitions are highly emotionally charged and therefore resistant to logical and collaborative problem-solving. It's very difficult to get an objective analysis of an issue when you feel a highly emotional commitment to something or someone other than the issue itself.

Such votes endanger school district alignment because they result in decisions that aren't consistently based upon a previously agreed-upon strategic vision. Partisan commitments are stronger than commitment to a larger vision—if vision exists at all in a partisan board environment.

Board partisanship will bring school improvement to a grinding halt and cause consternation at the tactical and operational levels. To tactical and operational staffs, there's no decision-to-decision flow; the board's strategic decisions have become haphazard, even if they are predictable given the known coalitions.

In short, the board's decisions need to be driven only by its strategic vision and the resulting school district's goals. Partisanship signals board trouble.

No single decision is as important for the board as is demonstrating, through its public actions and communications, that it's committed first and foremost to providing clear strategic leadership and direction to the school district. People will judge the board on *how* it provides that clear strategic direction far more than on *what* it decides.

#2 Not Supporting a Majority Board Decision

A healthy board response to a split vote is simply to move on to the next item for consideration. But if board members don't unanimously and sincerely back the majority's decision, no matter what their previous antipathy toward it was, then they're destabilizing the entire organization from the top down. The many tactical and operational people in the school district can't even have confidence that one or more board members won't sabotage a board decision. Organizationally, they're now on a rudderless ship in high seas—and they know it, though they likely won't directly state their fears to board members themselves because those members are terrifying them in terms of what might happen next. Yet board members will likely see none of this reaction. After all, who's going to tell the board, "You blew it"?

The time for a productive board debate is before *an issue is decided, not after.* Board members have the responsibility to discuss and debate issues prior to making decisions. Once they've made a decision, board members' most important responsibility is to provide stability and strategic clarity to the rest of the school district by publicly and privately supporting that decision—regardless of the issue or how they arrived at the decision.

To board members who don't want to support a majority board decision, we offer this basic and blunt advice: Get over it! It's crucial for the board to show a united front so that other roles, as well as the public, can rely on what has been decided. A ripple of discontent among some board members at a public meeting can generate a wave of concern at the tactical level and a tsunami of anxiety at the operational one. It's far better for staff members to spend their limited time improving the school district than coping with anxiety.

#3 Responding to Community Discontent Without Data or Process

Most boards experience community discontent at one point or another. The many stakeholder groups to whom the board is answerable have a wide variety of perceptions and opinions, and boards can't realistically represent them all in each decision. Some boards encounter only a little discontent from relatively few constituents, while others experience a lot from many. At times, the public can be dissatisfied with even the most competent and collaborative of boards.

What matters is not the discontent per se, but rather whether the discontent represents few or many stakeholders. If the board continually reminds the public of its overall strategic vision and ties each decision to that vision, it will eliminate *widespread* discontent. Relatively isolated discontent from a few, though certainly not desirable, is not nearly as significant, nor as long-lasting.

A tough thing for board members to figure out is when discontent constitutes legitimate feedback on board or organizational improvement, as opposed to when it's only a personal issue that the board can't or shouldn't address. How does the board sort through critical stakeholder feedback to determine what's worthy of its attention?

Parents or other community members usually are the primary constituent groups that express discontent to board members. Board members hear, directly or indirectly, complaints about either the people in the school district or the quality of the school system. Most members of the public are surprisingly effective in convincing a board member that a perceived problem is real. At times, it is, but at other times it isn't.

How can you tell? First, ask staff to investigate the issue. Beyond this, there are two approaches the board should take to sort through critical feedback:

1. Don't trust your ears alone.

2. Validate through data.

Don't believe all of what you hear; much of it isn't significant to your strategic vision. Sort through critical feedback to determine what is significant and what isn't by using your board experience, listening skills, role understandings, analytic abilities, and instincts. For example, you might trust what your neighbor says because you like and respect her. But trusting your ears alone isn't a reliable method to determine whether her complaint is valid. Remember, you possess limited tactical and operational insight, and much of what your neighbor is complaining about is beyond your direct knowledge or experience—and hers. Your familiarity with your neighbor doesn't necessarily mean that she's a source of reliable information, though she may be honest and sincere.

As the critical feedback gets louder and comes from more people and directions, it becomes harder to ignore, but that doesn't necessarily indicate that it's accurate. You must validate complaints before you "buy into" them. If a statement of discontent matches available data, then it's probably legitimate feedback worthy of the board's attention. But there may not be available data by which to validate it, or the complaint may not seem valid when held against the data at hand.

In general, you'll find it far easier to give a thoughtful response based upon data than based upon your intuition, feeling, or belief. The person who offers critical feedback might not like your response but will likely accept it better if you present it using objective sources rather than subjective feelings or opinions.

Once data have validated a complaint, the board should determine whether to direct time and resources to address it within the school district's present goals and strategic plan, whether addressing it will require formulating a new goal, or whether, despite its legitimacy, it should be addressed at all.

Even if the board deems a complaint legitimate, *the legitimacy of a complaint doesn't define how high a priority it should have.* The board has to assign a priority by weighing the importance of addressing the complaint against meeting the district's goals. After all, not enough time and resources exist to address everything that's worthy of being addressed, so the board must always pick and choose to avoid taking on too many things to do any of them well.

Based upon what it has found to be a legitimate complaint, the board may decide to adopt a new goal. That likely means that one or two existing ones will have to go, as the time and resources available to meeting existing goals haven't expanded because a new one has been adopted. More likely, the board will tell the person who brought the complaint that his or her issue, while legitimate, doesn't rise to the level of the goals which the board had adopted. If the organization's goals have previously been highly visible to staff and others in the school community, this response may suffice. But if the goals aren't well known, this answer likely won't be as satisfactory.

Basing board responses to public discontent on its strategic plan and on data related to the issue at hand has three implications:

1. Board responses will be more objective and more tied to existing organizational initiatives.

2. The more good data that the board has at its disposal, the easier it will be for it to respond objectively to criticism. Subjective board opinion isn't as convincing as objective data.

3. The board's response to the person who brings the complaint won't always be prompt, but it will be objective and methodical because research will inform it. A quick response is the intuitive reaction because it makes you feel that the discontent will go away. But in reality, such a response usually escalates the discontent because respondents don't perceive it as sincere or convincing.

The content of the board's response usually won't convince someone holding an opposite point of view. Aim toward having everyone respect a board's *process* of coming to a decision.

The sooner the board has good data at its disposal, the faster it can supply a thoughtful and objective response. Continuing failure to provide timely, objective responses to public criticisms signals that something is wrong with the way the board is functioning. This failure usually manifests by the board either becoming publicly and emotionally defensive about its decisions—reacting to public criticisms as if they were personal attacks—or just ignoring public criticism as if it had never occurred. Both reactions simply make the board's critics even more vocal and upset—not just about the precipitating issue, but also about the board's response or lack thereof.

What should board members do when public discontent is fierce? Sometimes, you simply have to "tough it out," especially when you have followed the strategic plan and used objective data. In such instances, the board must make a decision for the strategic good of the school district, even if staff or the public don't immediately understand or support that decision. The board's public role demands that you demonstrate sound strategic thinking and leadership. In the face of strong community opposition, your organizational goals and strategic plan are invaluable; in fact, without their guidance, the board probably will flounder in the face of strong community opposition.

The public measures the board's credibility, particularly at times of high public discontent, in three ways:

1. Its demonstrated ability to listen to opposing views in a sincere and open fashion
2. The quality (though not necessarily the content) of its response
3. Its ability to craft and deliver a quality response within a reasonable period of time

#4 Conducting Your Own Research

One of the administration's most important tasks is to conduct research that the board has requested. The administration has the necessary time, resources, and expertise for this work and also can coordinate the research undertaken by others and prepare it for board review in a timely fashion. When administrators lack technical expertise, their knowledge of the world of education allows them to identify outside experts who can produce quality research results.

What is the board's role in the collection of research? It isn't to perform research itself, particularly not by individual members, unless expressly invited to do so by the administrative staff. It also isn't to determine the tactics as to how the research will play out at the staff level. These are classic examples of board micromanagement of tactical responsibilities. It is instead to set standards for the quality of the research it expects to receive. The research process can be formal, such as investigating the professional literature on the effects of class size, or informal, such as speaking with parent groups to learn their views on class size. What's important is that staff members conduct the research or arrange for an outside expert to do it, and then develop the tactics for how the research will affect them. The results are then reported to the board.

Why shouldn't you conduct your own research? For example, you could do a website search on other school districts' lunch procedures or interview teachers and parents about school morale. Wouldn't that be a free service that would benefit the school district?

No, it wouldn't, because you'd be taking on tactical work independently of those who have the responsibility for doing research. In addition, your research might not be aligned to the strategic goals that the board has set. Finally, staff likely will be threatened by your independent research and view it as a board "fishing expedition," even if that's far from your intent.

The board member generally will attempt his or her own research for one of two reasons:

1. Conducting research is something the board member personally enjoys.

2. The board member doesn't trust the quality of the staff's research.

Neither reason justifies the act. The board member who enjoys conducting research still jumps out of a strategic role and into a tactical role. If a board member lacks confidence in the quality of the staff's research, he or she needs to take that concern to the full board, which should set clearer research standards or address a staff performance issue that the poor research has highlighted. But in neither case should the board member conduct the research himself or herself.

This isn't an issue about which role gets to conduct which research. It's about how a school district can best manage limited time and resources to move toward aligned improvement by assigning the responsibility of conducting all research to tactical staff. It's about finding organizational efficiency through common goals and tactics. Just as a well-meaning instrumentalist in an orchestra who isn't assigned a solo will cause consternation by spontaneously performing one, so will an individual board member by researching solo.

#5 Applying Expert Advice Literally Without Consulting Staff

Occasionally, the board or administration commissions an outside expert to provide an informed perspective on a topic or issue, often because someone in the school district desires "outside" advice. However, while an expert can give advice, he or she can't be as accurate in assessing the tactics required to translate recommendations into effective practice at a local level. In short, even if the expert provides sound advice about a particular topic, that advice might not work within a particular school district. For this reason, the board shouldn't apply an expert's advice without first consulting tactical and operational staff.

Boards and administrators need to set a high premium on getting everyone involved in and committed to what the expert recommends. It's no more acceptable for the board to receive an expert's advice and simply decree it as policy than it is for the board to decree as policy its own independent conclusions. At a practical level, while the board might want an expert's advice to be implemented, the administration must craft the tactics required to ensure teacher buy-in to the expert's message; only then will that message have a significant effect on the school district. *All three roles need to arrive at a consensus, as seen through their different lenses, before any significant or lasting change can occur in the school district.*

#6 Ignoring the Impact of Culture on Change

A school district's culture is a web of habit, understandings, and perceptions about "the way things have always been done around here." Staff members understand this culture intuitively; culture is the powerful glue that holds a school district together. In assessing the readiness of the school district to successfully embrace needed change, the board can't ignore the impact of culture.

The board can unwittingly cause cultural pushback that can delay or derail the implementation of its own strategic vision, even when that board is acting appropriately. For example, suppose that, to set strategic goals, the board has long utilized a strategic planning council that's comprised of board members, staff members, parents, other community members, and students. Of course, people expect the board to develop the next set of strategic goals in the same way. However, a newly seated board may decide that it wants to set the goals itself, without the help of a strategic planning council.

The board is perfectly within its role in making this decision; after all, it's responsible for setting the school district's strategic goals. But its decision-making process presents a major jolt to the existing school culture because it isn't "the way things have always been done around here." No one, besides the new board, knows why the organizational culture is being changed. The result? Pushback from people who were invested in the previous way of determining strategic goals and who aren't prepared for the cultural change—never mind that the goals this board chose are very good ones. The board could have avoided much of the pushback through some in-depth conversations about why it wanted to undertake the task of setting strategic goals itself.

People "push back" against change, particularly unplanned, random change, and the old culture may well strengthen in opposition as a result. Teachers push back through such statements as "Our plates are already too full." Pushbacks can be powerful and persistent because the randomness of change has made the culture more resistant to any change, good or bad.

Pushback is often hard for the board to read, but it always occurs for a reason. In this case, the board didn't properly assess the cultural dynamic of other people's investment in an established goal-setting process before it took action. Its decision-making process was not in alignment with the school district's cultural expectations. (See *Alignment Framework* in the appendix, page 138.)

The decision to hire a new superintendent is particularly important to align with district culture. We advise the board to gauge the impact of that culture before determining the attributes desired in the new superintendent. For example, if a popular superintendent leaves, people will want a continuation of what made the old superintendent popular, not a change in style and direction. But if stakeholders feel that the previous superintendent's performance was poor, they will more readily embrace a new superintendent whose values and beliefs align with those of the culture. If they don't align, the new superintendent's influence within the organization will immediately be compromised. It's not enough to choose a superintendent with whom your board is comfortable; you must also choose someone whom the culture will embrace. Seek someone who also wants to inspire and challenge the organization to continually improve. Change in school districts takes time even without leadership changes, and the district will need time to adjust to new leadership.

Culture will often be an impediment to continuous improvement—*until the organization embraces continual improvement as a core cultural value.* The cultural adoption of this value occurs over time, through strategically identified and gradually implemented changes.

Stephen Covey (1990) addresses the necessary linkage of organizational culture to change by observing that leaders need to be directed by core principles; these principles can guide leaders in the proper direction even when they are otherwise surrounded by confusing voices and messages. Covey also identifies the lack of shared values and vision as a chronic organizational problem that impedes the development of such principles.

Jeffrey Rosenthal and Mary Ann Masarech (2003) observe that "to develop a high-performance culture and organizational success, leaders must purposefully establish shared organizational values that guide behavior and influence practices" (p. 4). And Jack Canfield, Mark Victor Hansen, and Les Hewitt (2000) suggest that "core values serve boards as a litmus test that when something is done that contradicts these values, your intuition, or gut feeling, will serve as a reminder that something isn't right" (p. 69). Such values-based principles should guide the board's thinking, communicating, planning, and decision-making. They should be the metronome that defines the rhythms of the board's planning and decision-making.

Table 4-1 (page 74) gives examples of good core values that we adapted from Steve Benjamin's *The Quality Rubric: A Systematic Approach for Implementing Quality Principles and Tools in Classrooms and Schools* (2007).

Studer (2003) notes the importance of applying standards based on core values:

> We want to define more prescriptive actions that will drive results. We want to create enthusiasm for change, because change isn't easy. We want to help out our leaders by getting all staff on board early to engage them in the process. And we want to create systems and tools that will hardwire our focus on service . . . Most organizations have values statements, but they may not have very specific standards of behavior that clearly articulate how the employees will live out those values. (p. 75)

Studer stresses creating an organizational culture based upon the values of service and operational excellence. In so doing, it's critical that stakeholders both in and outside of the school system know exactly why the organization does what it does. They need and want to know what's going on; board members can "connect the dots" for them by making explicit the board's strategic vision and organizational expectations.

Any organization, including a school district, does this by establishing a *common organizational language*. For a school district, this occurs when all three roles say the same things in the same way to all stakeholders. This common organizational language clearly states organizational expectations, using the same words and phrases that cut across the otherwise different languages of the three roles discussed in chapter 3. In particular, the tactical and operational staffs need to know how the board's strategic direction will impact their work. Conversely, staff members should know how what they do connects with the school district's strategic direction and goals. Finally, organizational leaders need to recognize staff members who contribute to improved organizational performance and to challenge those who don't add value to the organization.

#7 Not Supporting District Policies

Most schools have a complaint process that begins closest to the point where the complaint took place and works its way up the role ladder to progressively higher levels of the school district for further consideration or appeal. This allows for progressive levels of review, but each level is further removed from the original point of issue and therefore less directly knowledgeable of the blend of facts and personalities that resulted in the issue emerging in the first place. In this sense, a complaint process is much like a legal appeals process, in which each subsequent review is more at the

Table 4-1: Core Values and Beliefs

Core Value	Definition
Alignment	Work together around common goals, and use common processes and measures to improve the school district's effectiveness and efficiency.
Leadership	Establish a vision of success, and organize the system so that it achieves success. Take responsibility for continuous improvement at your level of the organization.
High Expectations	Create a culture in which everyone strives to reach targets and, when they are achieved, attempts to "raise the bar" to continue progressing. Believe and act as if everyone can meet learning goals given sufficient time and resources.
Focus on the Vital Few	Emphasize the goals that are most important, and develop powerful strategies to achieve them. Pursue success relentlessly in a limited number of key performance areas.
Systems Thinking	Realize that complex systems are composed of many interrelated subsystems, that organizational effectiveness comes when all subsystems work effectively and harmoniously, and that poor performance in one area affects the whole organization.
Continuous Improvement	Manage the continuous improvement of processes and results through teams that meet or exceed stakeholder needs, and that do so through data-driven approaches.
Personal Accountability for Learning	Accept responsibility for achieving increased learning and other improvement goals that are appropriate for each person's role level. Learning occurs in typical environments such as classrooms and in continuous improvement teams.
Data-Driven Decision-Making	Use data and information, including measurement results and research, to choose the best responses to opportunities for improvement.
Teamwork	Achieve goals by forming groups of individuals with complementary skills.
A Focus on Results	Accept the importance of learning and performance outcomes as the key measures of an organization's success.

Adapted from: Benjamin, S. (2007). *The quality rubric: A systematic approach for implementing quality principles and tools in classrooms and schools.* Milwaukee, WI: American Society for Quality Press.

levels of precedent and process and less at the level of directly agreeing or disagreeing with the complaint.

A typical school district process will generally start with a resolution attempted at the classroom level (if the presenting issue is a classroom issue) or the principal level (if it's a school issue). Appeals are available at the principal (for classroom complaints), superintendent, and board levels, with the board having the final decision. In larger school districts, there may be other staff appeal levels—department heads between the classroom and the principal, or assistant superintendents between the principal and the superintendent—but the assumption of a prescribed hierarchy of appeal steps is the same. In all cases, appeals only go as far as they need to go to come to a resolution acceptable to both sides.

If the complaint process is followed, then all personnel in the school district, including the board, are operating appropriately within their assigned roles. When the board doesn't follow this process, this signals board trouble. What are some of the ways in which a board can get itself into trouble?

1. **Addressing a complaint personally.** This is easy to do, especially because a typical parent complaint—such as "My son's teacher doesn't call on him" or "The school keeps losing my daughter's lunch money"—doesn't sound very formal or complicated. An immediate solution seems easy—such as "I'll tell the teacher to call on your child" or "I'll get the school to refund your money"—while the complaint process seems too formal for such seemingly minor issues. But just because your response is easy doesn't make it right. And you're crossing roles—leaving your strategic role to address tactical or operational complaints.

2. **Creating an exception based on sympathy.** The board is the final arbiter not just for the individual complainant, but also for all similar complaints in the future. The board that makes a final decision based on personal empathy for a particular complainant decides, in effect, that his or her feelings are more important than the school district's procedures—particularly when these procedures were properly followed.

   If procedures weren't followed, the board should ordinarily side with the complainant for that reason. If procedures were followed, board members should support them because they're based on policies approved by previous boards and thus represent precedents that staff members can safely follow.

   The board *can* occasionally make a decision based on sympathy for the individual, but in so doing, it must take into consideration the wellbeing of all students, not just the individual's wellbeing. The board's strategic responsibility in instances like this is to ensure that its actions are aligned with the procedures of the school district; deviating from school district policies is a signal of board trouble.

3. **Enforcing a complaint process that seems flawed.** When your board confronts what seems to be a flawed policy, what should you do? If you decide to act in opposition to the existing policy, you need to know what changes to make in the policy to correct the flaws. Your board then needs to direct the administration to immediately craft a revision for prompt board review and adoption. If you don't take these policy steps and instead make a decision that violates your own policy, you create a dilemma for the administration: Does it follow the flawed policy, or violate the policy and try to guess the implications for future situations?

   It's a slippery slope for administration to try to craft its own policies "on the run," especially when the administration doesn't have the right to set policy. That right belongs to the board. The board must make sure administration enforces the policies the board wants enforced, but the board must first commit fully to the policies it already has.

4. **Undermining staff enforcement of board policies.** When the board becomes upset with administration for enforcing policies that the board doesn't favor, that's a signal of trouble not just for administration, but also for the board. The administration has a political problem: It's supposed to follow board policies, but the board won't support it if it does. Meanwhile, the board has a leadership problem: When it counters the staff's enforcement of board policies, it fails to give clear strategic direction. The board's mixed signals throw the entire school district out of productive alignment. The administration's political problem can only be resolved by having the board first clearly address its leadership problem.

#8 Failing to Foster a Three-Way Partnership With the Superintendent and Union Leaders

The board, the superintendent, and union leadership must establish a productive and professional three-way partnership for the school district to continuously improve. Make entering into such a relationship your primary goal, for without it, nothing you want to achieve will happen, no matter how much time and energy your board puts into its work. The most important signal that the board is in trouble occurs when the board fails to foster a solid working relationship with the superintendent and with union leaders. When all three parties aren't working together smoothly, too much time will be spent trying to resolve their differences and not enough will be spent working together to achieve the school district's strategic goals; any forward momentum will be halted.

Of course, even in the best of board-superintendent-union relationships, differences will occur. But in healthy relationships, each party demonstrates that it's willing to listen to and learn from the others, and the parties quickly resolve their differences in light of what will help the school district achieve its strategic goals.

The alternative is an emotional and adversarial relationship. If each party doesn't rely on objective criteria—the school district's strategic goals—in judging the others' actions, it will interpret those actions according to personal feelings. In short, emotion, rather than mutual respect, will define the board-superintendent-union relationship, which is a clear danger signal to the board that this most important of relationships isn't working. *When the board-superintendent-union relationship isn't working, nothing in the school district is working.* The battle between any two of the three parties will undermine confidence in the entire school district and bring into question its strategic direction. Each will be influential enough to stymie the others, but none will be strong enough to overcome the others and still allow the school district to move forward.

An important distinction among the three parties is that the board hires the superintendent, but inherits union leadership. Therefore, boards can fire superintendents, which makes the relationship between these two parties different from the relationship the board has with a union.

So decisions to terminate a professional relationship with the superintendent are based not so much on who's right or wrong, but rather on the board's decision to stop the battle. It can do so either directly, by firing the superintendent, or indirectly, by pressuring the superintendent to resign.

The board-superintendent leadership crisis must be resolved for the good of the entire school district and the community that supports it. This resolution can occur in one of three ways:

1. The board and superintendent reach agreement on their differences.

2. The superintendent leaves.

3. A new board that can partner with the current superintendent takes over.

Most differences between the board and its superintendent can be resolved if each side is committed to the school district's strategic vision and goals, has the skills needed for its role, and resists the temptation to micromanage. Otherwise, the board-superintendent relationship probably won't survive.

Notice that none of these three conditions addresses personality issues. While personality issues are common sticking points between the board and the superintendent, they become largely irrelevant if the three conditions for resolution are met. Personality-based issues create emotional criteria by which to judge a superintendent's performance, and issues that arise from them should instead be tied to objective performance criteria. What should ultimately matter most in the end is whether the superintendent contributes in a positive way, as determined by objective criteria, toward advancing the school district's strategic direction.

#9 Hiring a Superintendent on a Split Vote

The board should avoid hiring a superintendent on a split vote. A new superintendent will acquire immediate credibility according to the degree of public enthusiasm the board demonstrates in engaging him or her. If the vote to hire the new leader of the school district is split, people will ask, "What's wrong with this new superintendent that some members of the board don't want to hire him or her?" A split vote puts a new superintendent at an enormous initial disadvantage, especially if his or her charge is to promote change in the school district.

The hiring of a new superintendent is one of the few instances in which board consensus might not be desirable. If consensus requires that some board members have to "settle" for the least objectionable option, then chances are that the appointment of the new superintendent won't work out down the road. Given the importance of the board-superintendent working relationship, the board's choice of its new superintendent must be unanimous and enthusiastic if it's ultimately to be successful.

#10 Failing to Personally Detach From Board Decisions

Board actions can feel very personal; you make significant decisions and can feel very personally committed to them. Those board decisions couldn't have been made without you.

Of course, when you leave the board, someone else will be making those decisions with the same personal commitment that you had.

> You aren't the reason that board decisions are made, and such decisions aren't yours alone. In reality, you're a surrogate for the communities that support the school district. Therefore, the decisions you make aren't personal but are made on behalf of the organization as a whole, at all its levels.

Board membership is a much bigger role than any individual; it's a role for an entire organization that was functioning in the past, and will function in the future, without you. But for now, you, as the board member, have the opportunity to help shape in very important ways what the board does.

Good board members possess the ability to maintain some personal detachment from their decisions so as to ensure that such decisions are for the overall good of the organization, as opposed to merely fulfilling a personal belief or agenda. Failing to detach from board decisions is a trouble signal because only personal detachment ensures that board decisions are for the good of the school district.

Chapter Summary

#1 Engaging in Partisan Voting

- Idea-based votes send positive signals, while partisan votes send negative signals.

#2 Not Supporting a Majority Board Decision

- A board member's lack of commitment to a decision arrived at by a split vote is a major signal of board trouble.

- Tactical staff and operational staff react poorly to unaligned board behavior.

#3 Responding to Community Discontent Without Data or Process

- Widespread discontent is more dangerous than discontent from a few, regardless of the issue.

- In distinguishing legitimate discontent from all the public criticism the board will hear, it's much more effective to validate through data than to "trust your ears."

- Even if discontent is validated by data, the board must decide whether that discontent concerns a matter that falls within the district's strategic plan before expending time and resources to address it.

- The quality of the board's response to discontent is measured by the respect it gains for its decision-making process, not by what it decides.

- Although the board shouldn't substitute speed for methodical research in responding to a complaint, neither should it unduly delay a response.

- A complaint's legitimacy doesn't alone define its priority status.

- There are three implications to basing board responses to data and the strategic plan: (1) responses are more objective; (2) it's easier to effectively respond through good data; and (3) research may slow response time.

- The board that's continually frustrated about never having enough time is probably not using well the time it has.

- There are three elements that build public credibility: (1) how the board listens, (2) the quality of board responses, and (3) the timeliness of board responses.

#4 Conducting Your Own Research

- The board's role regarding research is to set quality standards, not to conduct research.

#5 Applying Expert Advice Literally Without Consulting Staff

- An expert's recommendations should only be implemented if all three roles agree on changes that will take place within the school district.

#6 Ignoring the Impact of Culture on Change

- The board must account for the school district's culture in setting strategic direction lest it inadvertently cause tactical or operational pushback.

- Adhering to core values is instrumental in creating a culture that can also accommodate change.

- Random changes, those unconnected to a unifying vision or plan, will likely cause organizational pushback.

- In choosing a new superintendent, board members should first "read" the school district's culture.

- New leadership usually needs time in order to establish itself and become effective.

#7 Not Supporting District Policies

- A good complaint process represents the needs of all three roles.

- Board members should remain within their strategic role by referring a complaint to the appropriate tactical or operational staff.

- Among the mistakes board members make in trying to resolve complaints is opposing policies they dislike rather than first trying to change such policies.

#8 Failing to Foster a Three-Way Partnership With the Superintendent and Union Leaders

- A poor board-superintendent relationship is a signal that the board is in deep trouble because such a relationship undermines the school district's efficiency and stops its progress.

- Performance evaluations should be based upon objective, goals-driven criteria rather than subjective feelings.

#9 Hiring a Superintendent on a Split Vote

- A split vote to hire a superintendent immediately compromises his or her credibility and ability to lead.

- Board consensus on the selection of a superintendent is not advised if some board members have to "settle" for the least objectionable option.

#10 Failing to Personally Detach From Board Decisions

- Board decisions aren't about you, but about everyone within and outside of the organization affected by those decisions.

- An aligned board member is a selfless strategic visionary.

5

Data: A Critical Tool for Your School Board

To make good strategic decisions, school boards need good information. Although this may seem an obvious fact, school districts often ignore it. Instead, they frequently make decisions based upon what is easiest to do, what costs the least, what "we've always done," or what they believe to be best. Occasionally, a little more rigor is applied to the process: "I heard about it at another school district," "I read that this approach is really good," "My best friend [or neighbor] swears by it," "This is what parents [or the community] want(s)." These decision-making rationales won't result in systematic choices that align school district initiatives because they lack an essential ingredient: good data. For our purposes, "data" refers to outcomes expressed numerically to show that something has happened (or not happened) as planned. A few examples of such data are student test scores, percentages based upon survey responses, budget information, demographic information on students, and types and numbers of courses offered.

Why are data good, and what makes it that way? Educational expert Mike Schmoker (1999) notes:

> Data can help us confront what we may wish to avoid and what is difficult to perceive, trace, or gauge: data can substantiate theories, inform decisions, impel action, marshal support, thwart misperceptions and unwarranted optimism, maintain focus and goal orientation, and capture and sustain collective energy and momentum. (p. 49)

Data are the only basis for objective decision-making. The alternative is decision-making driven by such subjective criteria as opinion, intuition, strongly held beliefs, habit, ease of effort, authority, political pressure, or the force of personality. Either way, decisions must and will be made.

Good data are fundamental to successful businesses, and some kinds of data are common in school districts. For example, school districts typically have good financial information and use it well. Most superintendents or business managers and many school boards can state the line-by-line details of their budget and where they stand relative to keeping monetary funds balanced. (That's largely because states require such reporting as a condition for allocating tax dollars and other state funds to local school districts.) In deciding a referendum, the public holds a school district's financial data to a high level of scrutiny. Referenda pass in part because of the clarity of good data that the public can easily understand.

In the No Child Left Behind era, student achievement data, usually derived from state test results, are under enormous scrutiny from all sides. A flood of such data is now available to schools, and the pressure "from above" that such data generate gets everyone's attention. But the question remains: To what extent do school districts use that information for proactive decision-making (as opposed to reactive, pressured responses)?

There are many reasons why it may seem that school districts should be exempt from detailed scrutiny of data. Unlike most private sector businesses, schools have no control over their "raw materials" (children), and the "product" they produce (educated citizens who contribute to a democratic society) isn't completed until long after students have left school. The school district also can't control the time a student spends outside of school, where school instruction can be either ignored or reversed.

Educational data can often appear maddeningly incomplete, particularly when they are compared to data in the manufacturing world, where such data routinely and quickly describe the quantity of the products, both manufactured and ordered; identify standardization criteria and production quality measures; and summarize the success of the company through its description of profits. Further, when compared to such fields as medicine, educational data are built upon relatively unscientific research, perhaps out of necessity. After all, who would be willing to allow his or her children to be the "control group" that doesn't receive the experimental intervention, or to take the placebo intervention that won't make a difference?

Finally, schools' educational efforts are usually measured by student test results, yet these results don't really determine whether a child will become a productive member of a democratic society, which is the big-picture goal for schools. Even the high-stakes tests that are driving public schools in the era of No Child Left Behind have huge time delays between testing and obtaining results. That makes it very difficult for school districts to recalibrate their efforts toward improvement in a timely way. In this sense, high-stakes testing has little chance for accurately predicting organizational improvement. While data can plausibly predict overall trend adjustments, data are at best imprecise in suggesting specific, targeted interventions that will guarantee success.

For these and other reasons, schools have often been resistant to using data to guide their decisions. NCLB has made such arguments irrelevant. Even given the potential imprecision of educational data, when educators use data with care and planning, they are still a more objective and truer guide for decision-making than the subjective alternatives.

And guess what? The right data really *can* make a difference in school improvement. Quint Studer (2003) elaborates:

> Organizations must be able to objectively assess their current status and then track their progress to the goals they have set. Measuring the important things helps organizations define specific targets, measure progress against those targets, and align the necessary resources to achieve them. Measurement supports the alignment of desired behaviors. It excites the organization when goals are achieved. Measurement holds individuals accountable for the results and helps to determine if things are working. Measurement aligns specific leadership and employee behaviors that cascade throughout the organization to drive results. (p. 61)

In short, using data well helps a school district stay on track and move forward, while misusing data can lead to misinterpretation, micromanagement, and bad decision-making. What data are selected for reports and presentations, how they are used, and who acts on what data will determine whether the data provide healthy, focused information for school improvement or whether they slow momentum and drain energy.

The Use of Data at the Three Organizational Levels

Board members: Data inform them as to the successes or failures of their strategic goals.

Administrators: Data inform them as to the effectiveness of their plans.

Teachers: Data inform them as to whether what they are doing in class-rooms is changing student learning.

Leadership guru Peter Senge (1990) observes, "Organizations learn only through individuals who learn. Individual learning does not guarantee organizational learning. But without it no organizational learning occurs" (p. 139). In this chapter, we'll apply Senge's observation to the world of education and deal with such questions as:

- How does the board use data—and what kind of data should it use—to set its strategic vision and charges?

- To what extent should data drive decisions by the school district?

- What data do teachers and students use to track learning progress?

- How are data used to investigate and address what people think of the school district?

- How do data affect what the school district decides, purchases, develops, and assesses?

We believe that for both individual and organizational learning to occur, it's essential to obtain data that focus upon what the school district most wants to know about, improve, and celebrate.

The appropriate use of data is fundamental to creating an aligned school system. The right data replace sincerely held beliefs with objective analysis. Data allow staff to *know* instead of feel, believe, guess, or pretend; data allow the organization to focus scarce resources on something likely to work, rather than experiment with well-meaning but unproven possibilities. Good data help keep a school district on a steady path over time, rather than just hopscotch to each educational "new thing" that comes along.

Facing Fears About Being Data-Driven

Being a data-driven school district means using data as an objective measure to determine whether your organization is accomplishing its goals and achieving the changes it desires. (Of course, data aren't the *only* source of information to indicate this.)

Yet some stakeholders might not embrace the idea of schools being data-driven. Many parents might feel the reliance on data will somehow remove the spontaneity and creativity from learning to the extent that students can no longer enjoy their school experience. Some teachers might resist the use of data in decision-making because it challenges their own perceptions of what should be done in the classroom, or because it might take more time to analyze and understand than they have available. Parents and teachers remember their own school experiences both subjectively and selectively, and want their children or students to have a similar school experience (or the polar opposite of their own if it was an unsuccessful one). Since everyone was once a student, everyone has deeply held beliefs as to how school should be, based upon their own personal experiences. Seldom do those deeply held beliefs embrace reliance upon data.

> Data supply focus to what goes on in the classroom or district. Data do not stop creativity, but inform it. The combination of specific content knowledge, keen instinct, and good teaching experiences is crucial to effective instruction.

Certainly utilizing data to make decisions can become counterproductive if data are overused or poorly used. A medical analogy: Taking too much of the best medicine available for a particular disease can be dangerous, even lethal, but that doesn't mean such medicines shouldn't be used in proper dosages. Similarly, although data used to the exclusion of other inputs can be harmful, such data, when used appropriately, can reap tremendous benefits for schools.

Let's address some of the fears one at a time:

- *"School won't be fun anymore."* This belief confuses *fun* with *focus*. Data serve a diagnostic purpose by helping educators focus on what children need to learn in order to succeed. Fun should be something that's planned around a focused goal, not something that takes its place. Data don't eliminate having fun in the classroom. Education is fun when children are motivated to learn, regardless of the content or the focus of the instruction provided.

- *"Data will take the creativity out of my teaching."* That will be the case only if a teacher stops being creative. Data describe what should be taught, while creativity addresses the manner in which instruction takes place. The two aren't mutually exclusive; data don't stop creativity but inform it. One can be creative with or without addressing what is most important for students to learn. But it's much better for students when teachers combine creativity and knowledge derived from data.

- *"I already know what's going on in my classroom."* What a teacher knows from instinct and experience, when added to objective data, can make for powerful instruction. But that doesn't mean that what a teacher knows should replace objective data about student learning. Instinct and experience alone are a prescription for the status quo in an era when the status quo is no longer valued or acceptable.

Another medical analogy may underscore the value of data for teaching. When a patient visits a doctor, he or she wants the physician to be an accurate diagnostician, to be highly skilled in medical techniques, and to have a good bedside manner. For the patient, all three attributes are important, the first two vitally so. Similarly, a teacher needs to accurately diagnose students' learning needs, to be highly skilled in delivering instruction, and to have the ability to motivate children to want to learn (roughly the educational equivalent of a pleasing bedside manner).

Teachers are usually highly skilled in instructional technique and have good "bedside" manners. They have been professionally certified to be competent in pedagogic skills, and parents and others place a high premium on teachers' ability to motivate children to learn. But teachers traditionally have been less rigorous about using objective data diagnostically to inform their instructional decisions, unlike the medical profession, which demands a high degree of data-driven rigor as part of diagnosis. Like teachers, school boards should use data diagnostically in making their strategic decisions. After we briefly discuss what constitutes good data, we'll explore how boards can effectively use data to help them decide what strategic charges they should set and to determine the outcomes they wish to result from these charges.

Understanding What Constitutes Good Data

Good data align to the long-term strategic goals of the school district. A school district's challenge is to identify what kinds of data it needs to measure the success of plans to meet those goals. Three things characterize these data:

1. *The data must directly connect to the goal.* They must accurately measure progress toward achieving the goal. Too often, data are "fudged" because they are all that's available, even though they don't accurately measure what is sought about results. In such instances, it's better not to measure results at all than to draw conclusions from data that are unaligned to goals. Perhaps the goal could be revised to more realistically connect to available data until the school district can develop the capacities to generate better data. For example, if the goal is to ensure that a student demonstrates a year's growth in reading as measured on the state test, then the assessment data have to be represented by a growth score. *Growth* data must track the *same* student from one year to another. To compare this year's third-grade scores to last year's scores doesn't tell us if last year's students improved; that would be using inappropriate data to draw conclusions.

2. *The data must be available.* You can think of the best and most descriptive data imaginable, but if your district doesn't have the capability to produce them, then those data won't be available for board analysis. Of course, there's a danger that boards will choose to do nothing because the data that they have aren't good enough. It's far better for boards to choose a more modest goal with available data—even if limited—than to do nothing at all because the optimum data aren't attainable. As illustrated by the previous example, it's better to learn something from the lesser data you do have than to learn nothing at all from data you don't have.

3. *The meaning and purpose of the data must be understood.* An objective analysis of data doesn't mean that any individual's interpretation should be accepted without question, though neither can it be ignored. Different people will read the same data differently. Because the analysis of quantitative information often leads to a desire to obtain more data to answer questions that arise through the initial analysis of data, subsequent data analysis can become a paralyzing exercise of ever deeper "data digs" to find the most precise and accurate interpretation on which everyone will agree. Inevitably, however, these deeper digs usually just result in more questions about what the data really mean because everyone will not likely ever completely agree.

Edie L. Holcomb, in *Getting Excited About Data* (2004), suggests the following questions to build common understanding about the data analysis process:

- What do these data seem to tell us?

- What do they not tell us? What else would we need to know?

- What good news is there to celebrate?

- What needs for school improvement might arise from these data? (p. 118)

Therefore, the board's purpose in analyzing data should be limited to monitoring the implementation of its strategic charges and other decision-making around school district goals.

Correlative and Causal Relationships

One caution about data analysis: Don't mistake *correlative* relationships for *causal* relationships. In *correlative* relationships, data show connections between two things, but don't indicate whether one thing caused the other. Correlations mean someone needs to ask more questions and generate more data to find out the possible causes. In *causal* relationships, data indicate that one thing definitively caused the other. Many more correlative than causal relationships can be found in educational data.

Knowing the difference between correlative and causal relationships helps define data's quality. The quality of data matters because an apparently good decision based upon bad data is really a bad decision. Likewise, a bad interpretation of good data leads to a bad decision. Good data are essential to making good decisions, but they don't alone guarantee that good decisions will be made as a result.

Types of Data

There are all kinds of school district data. For student achievement alone, there are school-organization data, grade-level data, classroom or subject-area data, and individual student data, all broken out by economic, ethnic, and other subgroups. There are usually perception data taken from parents, students, staff, or community members. There are financial data. There are employee data on who has been hired and who has left the school district, what their professional backgrounds are, and how long they have been employed. With the flood of data available to the board of education, many school districts are rich in data volume, but poor in data quality; that is, more data are generated than can be analyzed to provide useful information.

Deborah Wahlstrom (2002) delineates three types of data: outcome or performance, demographic, and process. She notes, "All three are important, but we use them in different ways—and we get different types of information from each" (p. 24). As Table 5-1 shows, each category measures outcomes or traits based upon one of Wahlstrom's three types of data.

Table 5-1: Types of Data

Type of Data	Examples
Outcome/Performance— "What They Got" Show what students learned or achieved. Paint the overall student performance picture . Show whether there are indicators of learning achievement in the classroom, school, or district.	Percentage of students who meet or exceed state test expectations Percentage of students above or below the norm on standardized achievement tests Percentage of students who meet or exceed district formative assessment benchmarks Percentage of students who earn a D or an E/F in English Percentage of students who pass the schoolwide writing test
Demographic—"Who Got It" Describe the students included in the outcome data. Disaggregate information by race and ethnicity, gender, and/or socioeconomic status. Indicate whether there is equity among subgroup population defined below within the outcome measures.	Percentage of each ethnic group that meets or exceeds state test benchmarks Percentage of males and females who meet or exceed state test benchmarks Percentage of different socioeconomic groups that receive a D or an E/F in mathematics Percentage of special education students who meet or exceed district benchmarks Percentage of limited-English-proficiency students who meet or exceed district writing prompt test benchmarks
Process—How and Why They Got It Provide clues about why students achieved at the level they did. Note the impact of outcome and performance data. Guide toward improvement.	Percentage of time students spend writing Percentage of students who indicate that they enjoy writing Percentage of teachers trained in teaching and assessing the writing process Percentage of teachers trained in the use of writing rubrics Percentage of students who appropriately use the grade-level writing rubric

Source: Wahlstrom, D. (2002). *Using data to improve student achievement.* Suffolk, VA: Successline.

The flood of continual data collection can result in a sea of random data that are unaligned to the school district's goals or priorities—far too much for anyone to sift through. The result? Nothing gets analyzed, and this sea of data is for naught, even though it takes a lot of staff time and energy to generate.

While these three categories of data involve objective information, a fourth category, *perception data,* is based on subjective views, as typically derived from satisfaction surveys. Such data are helpful in determining how satisfied various constituencies (students, parents, staff, and community members) are with the school district. For the board of education, information about how people feel about the school district is useful, especially when compared to objective data. Perception data answer the question: Are people's perceptions aligned with the board's attempts to improve the organization?

Internal and External Comparisons

When analyzing the four kinds of data, your board might engage in either internal or external comparison. *Internal comparison* looks at whether your school district is improving or slipping compared to how it did in the past. *External comparison,* also called *benchmarking,* occurs when the school district compares its performance to that of other school districts. Benchmarking can be a powerful data tool to drive school improvement. Boards should consider utilizing comparative data and benchmarking against similar or higher performing school districts to drive improvement efforts in a focused, aligned way.

In sorting through all available data, your board should address two questions:

1. Which data align to school district goals?

2. For what purpose does the board want to examine data? For strategic, tactical, or (less often) operational understanding?

Which Data Align to School District Goals?

School district goals determine the answers to the first question, as shown by the following examples:

- If the board wants to know how all students are achieving around established learning benchmarks, it should focus on academic data. If the board wants to see improvement among its populations at risk, it should focus on data from that subgroup.

- If the board wants to know how parents, students, and staff view their school experiences, it will want to see perception survey data.

- If the board wants to know when it is likely to run out of money, it will need multiyear financial projections.

- If the board wants to know if it has enough space in its buildings, it will want to see class-size breakouts and school use plans.

For What Purpose Does the Board Want to Examine Data?

The answer to the second question depends on whether the board uses data to inform strategic decisions or to supply tactical or operational background. (The board rarely has use for operational student achievement data generated at the individual student or classroom level.) Background information on tactical matters provides context that leads to more informed strategic board decision-making. However, that same information can be dangerous if it's used to justify board micromanagement of tactical planning.

Boards should examine data that are aligned to school district goals to judge how successful the organization has been in meeting the strategic targets that the board has set. But to understand the context in which tactical and operational staff work, the board may also want to see school-level or even grade-level data. The examination of data on significant subsets of the school district can be an important part of the board's appropriate monitoring of how well the organization is doing. But this examination of data shouldn't lead the board to start crafting tactical plans, for it must stay true to its strategic responsibility.

The Line Between Strategic and Tactical Data

The board can determine the line between strategic and tactical data in how it responds to the data it sees. For example, if the board examines information that indicates that two of its seven schools (A and D) show academic achievement at significantly lower levels than the other five schools, it might conclude that the curriculum of the two lagging schools needs more rigor. If the board wants to make a *full organizational response* to this data, it will set a strategic charge that increases the curriculum's rigor in all seven schools, including A and D. Should the board focus on increasing the curricular rigor in only the two schools, then its charge ceases to be strategic and instead becomes tactical, meaning that the board is engaging in micromanagement.

Why? By focusing only on schools A and D, rather than on all seven schools, the board has imposed two (rather than one) sets of curricular standards for the school district—a remedial charge for schools A and D and a separate charge for the other five schools. Instead, the board should have applied one charge strategically—to all seven schools—and left to the administration the task of planning how interventions might differ in schools A and D. Only by making a full organizational response to data can the board stay within its strategic role. When it starts to address issues concerning particular subsets of the organization, it strays into the tactical role.

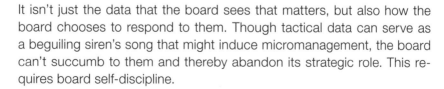

It isn't just the data that the board sees that matters, but also how the board chooses to respond to them. Though tactical data can serve as a beguiling siren's song that might induce micromanagement, the board can't succumb to them and thereby abandon its strategic role. This requires board self-discipline.

Understanding the Value of a Strategic Plan

Once quality data are in place, that data will drive the school district's future direction. It is through the collection, analysis, and reporting of the right data that the board sets future direction. An important tool for the board to use to stay strategic is a long-range plan.

Significant school district change is difficult at best, but it's impossible without solid community backing. A strategic plan sets a long-term vision that the public embraces because its representatives were involved in developing that plan. This process gives the board a solid political base on which to set goals for improving the school district. An astute board will leverage community involvement as it creates and carries out goals linked to the strategic plan. At its meetings, the board can use data to support its case and thereby build upon that initial wellspring of community support.

A strategic plan reinvigorates the school district by putting forth a vision of a better future. The board's presentation of the strategic plan offers an ideal time to introduce more systematic rigor to the school district. One data-based way to do this is by introducing SMART goals to the organization's schools.

For a graphical representation, see *Strategic Plan Flowchart* in the appendix (p. 140).

SMART Goals

Jan O'Neill and Anne Conzemius (2006) define a SMART goal as Specific and Strategic, Measurable, Attainable, Results-based, and Time-bound; Table 5-2 (page 91) summarizes their findings.

SMART goals at a school level are determined after site staff completes a data analysis process that identifies those areas most in need of schoolwide improvement. SMART goals are set by requiring improvement for the identified areas, and each improvement step is made a *reachable* possibility. This process will build the staff's commitment to data-driven continuous improvement. *Small incremental improvement steps, successfully attained, will lead to continuous improvement over time.*

The board approves SMART goals after staff reviews and makes recommendations about the goals' language. Boards can learn three valuable lessons from the way these goals are constructed and assessed:

1. SMART goals set measurable targets that are described by specific data that are to be collected.

    An example of a measurable target is: "Eighty-three percent of the eighth-grade algebra students will score an 85% or better on the second quarter end-of-the-unit test." The board should do the same with its strategic goals by setting targets that represent the measurable changes it expects to be achieved within a given period of time. The board's counterpart to this example might read: "The number of algebra students who attain a B or higher average for the year will increase by 5% from the previous year" or "The number of eighth graders enrolled in algebra will increase by 3% from the previous year."

Table 5-2: SMART Goals

Characteristic	Definition
Strategic and Specific	Focus on the vital few high-leverage areas where the largest gaps between vision and current reality exist.
	Align your goals as a system to drive resources and attention toward improvements.
	Focus on specific targets for improvement.
Measurable	Create multiple measures for each goal.
	District goals focus primarily on summative measures, while classroom-level goals should be both summative and formative in their focus.
	District use the data to adjust resources, programs, schedules, staffing, and so on, while teachers use the data to improve their practice, provide feedback to students on their learning, and summatively record student mastery.
Attainable	People need goals worthy of their commitment.
	Goals that motivate us to strive higher are those that are almost, but not quite, within our reach—that we need to stretch to achieve.
	Attainability is very much correlated with how large the gap is that we want to close and how much focus, energy, time, and resources we are prepared to put into attaining the goal.
Results-Based	We have concrete benchmarks against which to measure our efforts.
	When we ground goals in results, we build in immediate feedback that supports our sense of efficacy.
Time-Bound	Setting a goal that is time-bound builds internal accountability and commitment.
	If you did not meet your goal within that timeframe, then you would have an opportunity to learn why you did not and make adjustments.

Source: O'Neill, J., & Conzemius, A. (2006). *The power of SMART goals: Using goals to improve student learning*. Bloomington, IN: Solution Tree Press (formerly National Educational Service).

2. The targets are set to be attainable within prescribed time periods.

    This point is vital. The philosophy behind a continuously improving system is that the system always needs to improve and the staff needs to feel hopeful that ongoing improvement is possible. In their zeal to make changes quickly, boards may set targets that are unattainable, at least within the time prescribed for needed change to occur. (Remember, boards tend to have very short timeframes for organizational change). If tactical and organizational professionals don't feel the goals are within their grasp, their commitment to these goals will die. The practical implication is that board goals should be negotiated with tacticians so that the targets are viewed as challenging but attainable. *Striking this balance between challenging targets (the board's concern) and attainable targets (administrators' and teachers' concern) is crucial to setting appropriate strategic goals.*

3. The strategic goals are data-driven expressions of what the board believes should be the most important areas of focus for the school district.

    Boards need to keep this in mind as they confront other issues and concerns, which by definition are supposed to be less important. If the strategic targets are met, the school district has succeeded in addressing the board's most important concerns.

No one at any level should have to guess at or be surprised by what is strategically most important to the school district, especially when targets can be clearly defined through the use of data. When the board stays focused on these strategic goals, tactical and operational staff know up front what is of primary concern rather than having to react to what may seem like ad-hoc decisions.

While the board should *monitor* progress in attaining strategic goals, it shouldn't substitute or add its own board goals that compete for the school district's time and resources.

Using a District Performance Scorecard

The board needs a simple, standardized format by which to organize and to effectively and transparently communicate to its staff and the public its strategic goals and progress toward meeting them. The preferred format is a district performance scorecard; it takes the board's strategic goals and converts them into a succinct document for both board and public purposes.

Just as a student report card documents the learning that the child has mastered in a given period of time, so a district performance scorecard reports on whether the school district has met the board's strategic goals. And just as a student report card has letters or numbers that reflect grades, so a district performance scorecard contains metrics (measurements) that reveal the extent to which the school district has achieved its strategic goals (see appendix, *Scorecard Metrics*, p. 141).

However, a student report card is incomplete without contextual information to help parents understand the grades. Similarly, a district performance scorecard requires backup materials to provide clearer meaning to its metrics. What follows is an example of a fictional district performance scorecard, along with explanations of key symbols. It represents a *district* summary of a full school year through numbers that the board feels represent its strategic priorities. No individual school measures are represented in this scorecard example.

Table 5-3: District Performance Scorecard

Priority/Aim	Indicators	When	B	G/T	C
Student Achievement Annually improve student performance in literacy and numeracy.	ISAT Reading/Math 3–8	Annually	73/82	78/87	74/88
	ACT 11	Annually	60	66	60
	Graduation Rate	Annually	77	83	80
	NWEA Reading/Math Growth 3–7	2x Year	45/49	55/58	48/52
	Local Benchmarks Elem K–5/ 6–8	Trimester	66/55	72/65	73/63
	Local Benchmarks High 9–12	Semester	53	60	55
	Achieve. Benchmarks Read	Annually	4/12	2/12	4/12
	Achieve. Benchmarks Math	Annually	3/12	2/12	2/12
	Achieve. Benchmarks Sci	Annually	3/12	2/12	2/12
Safe & Nurturing Environment Continuously provide a safe and nurturing climate.	Discipline Suspens./ Expuls. Middle/High	Annually	.69/.93	1%/1%	.73/1.4
	Disc. Class 2–3 Referrals Middle/High	Monthly	27/39	20/25	23/31
	Class Size PK–2/3–5/6–12	2x Year	23/25/27	23/25/27	22/25/28
	Organ. Health Elem/ Middle/High	Annually	63/57/51	75/75/75	70/65/59
	Facility Assessment Elem/ Mid/High	Quarterly	78/71/65	80/80/80	75/77/68
	Facility Usage Elem/ Middle/High	Annually	98/95/90	95/95/95	100/95/93

continued on next page →

Priority/Aim	Indicators	When	B	G/T	C
Fiscal Health Annually maintain highest "recognition" status on the state financial profile.	State Annual Financial Report	Annually	3.5	4.0	4.0
	Audit	Annually	none	none	none
	3-Year Projection (Ed Fund)	Annually	43	30	51
	3-Year Projection (Combined)	Annually	45.5	30	53
	Budget to Actual (Ed Fund)	Quarterly	103/99	+/- 2%	103/98
	Budget to Actual (Combined)	Quarterly	103/98	+/- 2%	103/97
Customer Service Continuously improve satisfaction of students, parents, and community members.	Student Satisfaction Elem/Middle/High	Annually	86/77/75	85/85/85	88/81/80
	Parent Satisfaction Elem/Middle/High	Annually	88/81/75	85/85/85	85/80/81
	Community Satisfaction	Bi-Yearly	83	85	83
Quality Personnel Annually attract and retain quality personnel.	Staff Satisfaction Elem/Middle/High	Annually	79/71/67	85/85/85	82/79/77
	Board Certified Elem/Middle/High	Annually	8/5/12	20/20/20	10/7/15
	Retention Elem/Middle/High	Annually	85/81/80	90/85/85	88/82/78

Note that the scorecard itself is a one-page document with columns that identify strategic priorities and categories of general areas of school district focus ("priority and aim"). "Indicators" tell what subsets from each category are to be measured, and a "when" column that specifies the frequency with which an indicator will be measured. These are followed by three columns of metrics that describe a "baseline" ("B") or beginning measurement, a target ("G/T" or Goals/Targets) measurement that indicates the level of improvement desired, and a "current" ("C"), or most recent, measurement. For ease of interpretation, the "C" column should be color-coded: green for meeting or exceeding the target, yellow for staying at or improving from the baseline but not attaining the target, and red for falling below the baseline.

By viewing this graphic, color-coded document, anyone can quickly tell where the school district stands at a given time in terms of attainment of strategic goals and improvement of the school district. (See *District Performance Scorecard* and *Scorecard Backup Data* in the appendix, p. 142 and 145, for complete examples.)

Two important scorecard requirements are as follows:

1. The scorecard itself should be concise—as close to one page as possible.

2. Each indicator should be given only one metric, meaning one cell in the table.

Making the scorecard succinct forces the board to identify a limited number of important strategic goals that the organization will have adequate time and resources to address. A concise scorecard also makes the reporting of progress toward achieving board goals easier to understand for the school district's staff and the public.

Using the Right Data for Different Roles

Each role requires data suited to its responsibilities. The use of this specifically chosen data is the means by which the board can determine whether the school system is aligned.

If data expressions beyond the district level—school, grade-level, or classroom data, for example—don't belong in a district performance scorecard, are they available anywhere else in the school district?

They are—in fact, they must be—if the school district is to meet its long-term strategic goals and if the board is to properly demonstrate its strategic leadership. But those deeper data analyses will occur where those data are the most useful and appropriate. *Appropriate* is the key word; it means that there's a legitimate function for the data at that level, and their use is respectful—the information won't compromise staff privacy or expose anyone to inappropriate scrutiny.

The same data can be appropriate at some levels of the school district and inappropriate at others. For example, consider the issue of identifying students by name in reports of individual assessment scores. Of course, it's appropriate that each student know his or her score, but it's inappropriate that the student know the score of every classmate. And while it's appropriate that the classroom teacher know all of the student names that are linked to particular scores, such detailed information is inappropriate as part of the backup data in a district performance scorecard.

Align Data Through Six Levels of the School District

Figure 5-1 (page 97) shows how data can align through six different levels of a typical school district. Rick Stiggins (2006) provides the central concept driving this premise—that there are different data suited for different levels and that data not appropriate for some levels are appropriate for other levels:

Productive assessment systems must serve many users. Decision makers at all levels need access to a variety of different kinds of information in different forms at different times. If any information user's needs are ignored, or if the decision is provided with information from inept assessments, ineffective decisions will result that will harm student confidence, motivation, and learning, as well as teaching efficacy. (p. 5)

Figure 5-1 shows six levels of a typical school district: student, classroom, grade or subject, school, district, and board. All six levels need data, but the kind each needs, while similar in indicator, is different in detail. For example, if the common indicator for all six levels is state reading scores, at the student level, there are individual reading scores for that student. At the classroom level, there are individual scores for each student in the classroom as well as a classroom average.

At the grade or subject level, there are reading scores that represent all students in the grade or subject area broken into reading categories, such as general comprehension, meaning, vocabulary, inferences, and extended responses. At the school level, there are reading score averages or ranges for the whole site, perhaps broken out by site, subject area, or subgroup, but never by student (or teacher) name. Here, the data take the form of a school performance scorecard, which is similar to in format and aligned through the metrics chosen with a district performance scorecard.

At the district level, there are similar breakouts of reading data across all schools. At the board level, the data will take the form of a district performance scorecard. Reading scores, for example, will be organized by grade clusters—primary, intermediate, middle school, and high school averages or ranges. There can also be districtwide demographic data that cut across all schools or subject area clusters with the same kinds of breakouts. These breakouts can be in the form of internal (within district) or benchmarking (across-districts) comparisons.

Figure 5-1 illustrates that there are also different data *formats* appropriate for different levels. For example, at the student level, data are displayed through a student data folder containing individual data on schoolwork that the student collects and tracks through student-made graphs and charts. For example, a student might graph his math quiz results or chart her reading scores or the books she's read during the year.

Figure 5-1 also shows the differing *purposes* for which data are used at different levels of the school district. For the student, the data's purpose is to "own your own learning" by assessing progress through a student portfolio (see *Student Data Folders* in the appendix, page 146) and setting self-developed goals for learning improvement. For the teacher, the data's purpose is to determine how close students are to achieving schoolwide learning goals and to understand how to adjust instruction to better meet student learning needs (see *Classroom Communication Boards* in the appendix, page 136).

At the grade or subject area level, the data's purpose is to help teacher teams to get information about how to help each other with different instructional strategies and ideas. At the school level, the data's purpose is to monitor progress toward some common school achievement goals. At the district level, it's to determine how financial and other resources can be better aligned to the strategic goals of the school

Level	Student	Classroom	Grade Level or Subject Area	School	District Office	Board
Data Formats	Student Data Folder	Communication Board	Communication Board	School Performance Scorecard	District Performance Scorecard backup prep, demographic, grade level, subject area breakouts	District Performance Scorecard and backup
Data Expressions	Individual student data	Individual student data by classroom	Student scores across grade level or subject area	Student score averages, ranges by grade, subject area, demographic	District score averages, ranges by grade, subject area, demographics, schools	District score averages by clustered grades, district demographics
Purposes	"Own Your Learning"	Inform classroom instruction; monitor school goals progress	Share instructional strategies; monitor school goals progress	Monitor school goals progress	Align resources to learning needs	Report to community; monitor strategic goals progress
Alignment Path				Monitor school-wide needs, targets	(Multiple schools)	Set strategic priorities

Figure 5-1: Data aligned across system levels.

district. At the board level, the data's purpose is to monitor and report to the public on progress toward achieving the district's strategic goals.

Monitoring Progress and Comparing Performance Results

A district performance scorecard and its backup data are powerful tools, but they must be used carefully. When used without thoughtful advance planning, they can cause considerable damage within and outside of the school district by:

- Creating additional tactical mandates that don't align with other mandates or with existing strategic goals

- Using precious organizational time and resources on initiatives that aren't strategically important

- Reporting to the public on data that don't represent mutually agreed-upon strategic initiatives, thereby creating community expectations for things that haven't been designated as strategic priorities

By operating in a transparent way and sharing with staff and the public its strategic goals and the metrics by which it will measure success, the board must walk a fine line. It needs to inspire staff members toward continual improvement without making them feel that they can't succeed or that they are to blame for failure to meet strategic goals beyond their control.

The board must also examine how resources are deployed and assess whether it needs to redistribute them to focus more effectively on strategic goals. In addition, the board must make sure that a change in resources won't cause so much upheaval in the school district as to draw vital time and energy away from meeting those goals.

Finally, the board must inspire the community to believe that the board can take a school district that the public perceives as good and make it better. The board needs to do so without making the community believe schools need so much improvement that people lose faith in the school district—and thereby the school board—that things can ever significantly become better. A good way to accomplish this is to partner with tacticians and community advisory groups in delivering the board's messages of improvement.

The board must be aware of the potential that its intent can always be misconstrued and so must craft its strategic messages to show understandings of tactical and operational concerns and overall community aspirations. Although it has powerful data tools like a district performance scorecard and backup data with which to craft its messages, the board needs to realize that these tools can just as easily cause misunderstanding about the board's motives and intent.

> An astute board will spend much of its time considering how to craft and deliver its messages in collaborative and supportive ways, even as it promotes more challenge and rigor for the school district. Such collaborative and supportive communication will assuage the natural concerns and fears of staff and parents about basic institutional change.

How the scorecard's goals are applied and how targets are reached are tactical and operational responsibilities, not strategic responsibilities. By reviewing scorecard reports, the board can monitor the results of these tactical and operational tasks, but the tasks themselves belong to staff. For example, the board can ask administrators to share their tactical plans to meet scorecard targets, but shouldn't dictate those plans. Once the board has set clear targets, it's up to staff to meet them or to explain with data why they weren't met.

A well-crafted district performance scorecard is public, clear, and transparent; it keeps what's most important to the board in the staff's and the public's eye and is almost impossible to misconstrue. Once the scorecard is adopted, competent tactical and operational administrators will welcome the clarity and guidance it provides.

> Boards should work collaboratively, particularly with staff, but also with the community, in setting strategic goals. It's easy to gain commitment from those who are directly involved in a goal-setting process.

Take Incremental Steps

In utilizing a district performance scorecard, the school district is committing to taking incremental steps toward meeting strategic targets. As long as the general trend is toward meeting goals (turning the scorecard more green than red or yellow), the school district is making suitable progress.

It's better to institute ongoing improvement over time than to push for one grand change overnight. Continuous school improvement isn't about making a specific change faster than scheduled, but about making incremental changes steadily and regularly. Continuous improvement isn't a sprint; it's a never-ending marathon.

How does the board ensure the proper interpretation of the district performance scorecard to both staff and the public? It does so through tracking progress toward the goals through periodic updates of the scorecard and through comparing results, as expressed through data, to preestablished targets.

The board needs to exercise *oversight* through ongoing scorecard reviews based upon the frequency (the "when" column) with which the data are collected. This means the scorecard should have a mix of annual and more frequent data checks and a diverse mix of indicators, particularly for student achievement measures, because no single measure will give an accurate summary of student learning. Although the scorecard measures progress toward meeting multiyear strategic goals, it measures this progress on an annual or more frequent basis. That's because you can only measure long-term progress by assessing the effectiveness of short-term incremental steps. In a continually improving school district, measuring the effects of these steps becomes a way of life.

Annual measurements alone are too infrequent. The scorecard, while certainly containing some annual measurements, should also have more frequent ones, so that the monitoring of progress can occur in an ongoing way and adjustments can be made more frequently than annually. For example, along with an annual state exam that measures student achievement, there should be more frequent (semiannual or quarterly) ways to assess it. In this way, the timing of what data are collected when will lead to a regular schedule of board monitoring and tracking.

If a district performance scorecard represents what's most important to the board, the oversight of this scorecard should be a featured part of each board meeting (see *District Scorecard Calendar* in the appendix, page 147). This process demonstrates to the community that the board takes seriously its responsibility to monitor what it's deemed most important. The scorecard also will provide the public with ongoing, easily digestible information about how progress in a complex organization is actually taking place.

Schedule the oversight during the month when it's most appropriate to monitor and report a change in data. For example, the financial data should be reported during budget time, the achievement data during the month when state achievement scores are released, and the customer satisfaction data during the month when the survey data are released. Function, rather than the scorecard, should drive any data collection schedule. Scorecard reporting then adapts to that schedule.

During the oversight process, board discussions need to focus on understanding the changes being attempted in the school district and deciding whether the board's initial targets seem realistic given current tactical and operational realities. The board also should engage in an ongoing conversation with staff, particularly administration, about what it will take to make these changes really happen. The board's role is to assess whether reasonable progress is being made toward reaching a goal, not to promote a race against the clock in terms of the original goals and timelines set.

Consider Context

In comparing performance results, particularly across schools or school districts, bear in mind four considerations:

1. Don't compare different kinds of things as if they were the same.

2. Good data access and retrieval become a focus for resource deployment decisions.

3. Not every attempt at improvement has to be successful; you can learn good things from unsuccessful as well as successful attempts.

4. Data comparisons can confuse a focus toward organizational change with evaluation of the people trying to attain the change.

Concerning the consideration against comparing different things as if they were the same, board members sometimes make the mistake of comparing two schools that not only have different student achievement results, but also different demographic, fiscal, or other realities that might help explain those results. It's inappropriate to compare those two schools simply on the basis of their achievement results when the schools themselves are different. Benchmark a school to others within or outside of the district that have similar demographic and other attributes.

Through this kind of comparison, the board can receive a true "read" for the school and thus be better able to set attainable targets for it. An attainable target will likely not be the same for one local school as for another, unless many of the schools' demographic and other attributes are similar. In short, while it's easier for the board to simply compare student achievement data across schools without considering contextual information, such shortcuts won't lead to good or accurate conclusions.

Data are good when accurate, and test scores of students in individual schools usually are. But if you compare scores of students in two or more schools, the pooled data are inaccurate unless contextual data become part of the equation.

A district performance scorecard, then, puts a premium not only on good data, but also on appropriate *contextual interpretations* of that data. One implication of improved data quality becomes apparent when the board considers how to deploy resources to meet its goals. Deployment decisions will increasingly focus on access to and retrieval of good data, and the personnel required to deliver it.

What if board targets aren't achieved and goals aren't met? Sometimes this occurs because staff didn't try hard enough to achieve them. But this isn't the typical reason goals aren't achieved. More likely, the targets weren't achievable given the time and resources committed to them, or the goals themselves were set too high. When either of these reasons occurs, the school district might learn from the experience in order to make its next attempt to hit the target more successful. A focused effort, even if unsuccessful, can result in a school district becoming more ready for and more informed toward what is needed to ultimately improve.

Thoughtfully analyze why a goal wasn't reached. Keep in mind that scorecard targets serve to determine what it will take to make real and lasting improvements in the school district; they aren't designed to be an accurate or effective instrument for evaluating tactical staff. The real focus of the board's monitoring through a district performance scorecard needs to be the organizational *change* being attempted, not the *people* trying to effect that change.

The focus upon organizational improvement is the core reason why the board utilizes a district performance scorecard. Organizational change is difficult; if it weren't, it would have occurred long ago through the efforts of previous boards and staff. And successful change is less about assessing staff effort and more about attaining learning results. This focus on what *learning results* children will derive from change needs to be the board's first and ongoing priority.

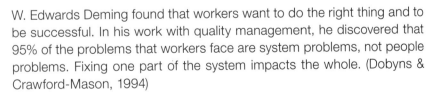

W. Edwards Deming found that workers want to do the right thing and to be successful. In his work with quality management, he discovered that 95% of the problems that workers face are system problems, not people problems. Fixing one part of the system impacts the whole. (Dobyns & Crawford-Mason, 1994)

Chapter Summary

- Each role—board, administration, teachers—requires data suited to its own responsibilities.

- Educational data have shortcomings but are still the best way by which to make objective decisions.

- Data are an essential ingredient for organizational alignment and replace unproven belief with objectivity.

Facing Fears About Being Data-Driven

- Data don't take the fun out of learning; they provide focus to what needs to be learned.

- Data don't prevent creativity; they inform it.

- Data don't diminish a teacher's instinct and experience; they add to his or her impact.

Understanding What Constitutes Good Data

- Data must be directly and accurately linked to the board's goals.

- The use of limited data is better than the use of no data at all.

- Good data analysis identifies what the data say *and* what they don't say.

- A decision based upon bad data is a bad decision, and bad interpretation of good data leads to a bad decision.

- Boards should ask two questions: "Which data align to board goals?" and "What's the data's purpose—strategic decision-making or contextual understanding?"

- Tactical data can provide the board with helpful background information, but they shouldn't lead to board micromanagement of tactical actions.

- Boards that make full organizational responses to data will likely stay strategic; boards that give charges to only some schools aren't making a full organizational response and will therefore make tactical rather than strategic decisions.

Understanding the Value of a Strategic Plan

- A strategic plan creates a firm political base for setting organizational goals.

- Like SMART goals for schools, board-designed goals need to (1) define what's most important for the school district, (2) state measurable targets, (3) be realistically attainable as well as challenging, and (4) prevent guessing by staff and the public as to the board's strategic priorities.

- In an aligned school district, the board shouldn't adopt its own medium- or short-term goals, unless they are in support of and aligned to long-term strategic goals.

Using a District Performance Scorecard

- The board's scorecard is a public report of its strategic priorities to staff and the community.

- When feasible, scorecards should be limited to one page, and indicators to one measure for baseline, target, and current metrics.

- Backup data to the scorecard are mainly intended to help the board analyze the scorecard's metrics, not to answer every board question that might arise.

Using the Right Data for Different Roles

- The same data can be appropriate at some levels of the school district and inappropriate at others.

- Data should align across all six levels of a school district.

Monitoring Progress and Comparing Performance Results

- The public and staff must accurately understand the board's strategic intent.

- Board communications should promote challenging and rigorous change through collaboration with, and the support of, staff and the public.

- Crafting a scorecard, which involves setting clear organizational targets, is the board's direct strategic responsibility. Setting the plans to achieve these targets is a tactical—not a strategic—responsibility.

- Board oversight—monitoring whether the school district is achieving scorecard targets— is a strategic responsibility.

- The board monitors a scorecard by how it tracks progress toward goals and how it compares results.

- Scorecard discussions should be a regular agenda item for board meetings.

- The analysis of scorecard results should always focus upon whether the original goals are currently attainable, given the organization's available resources to try to meet them.

- Achievement results among schools shouldn't be compared without considering demographic and other data issues.

- Good data access and retrieval increasingly become decisions for resource deployment.

- Even a failed attempt at improvement can be instructive in being better prepared for the next attempt.

- Comparative data should not be used for staff evaluation but rather for organizational improvement.

6

Four Common Issues in Board Service

In this chapter, we discuss four common issues that come before school boards to illustrate how the strategic and tactical roles can work in an aligned and coordinated fashion. We're not attempting to suggest that "one size fits all," for each situation that a board confronts is unique in terms of its setting, personalities, and the school culture. We also don't attempt to identify all the possible considerations that might arise for your particular school district.

Our focus in this book is on the board and its interaction with the superintendent and other tactical staff, but the operational role is just as important in contributing to a school district's success. No school district policies are likely to succeed, particularly with children at the classroom level, if your board hasn't first taken into account operational concerns. Although this chapter's discussions don't account for operational staff, student, parent, or community influences, these influences should be a legitimate part of a more thorough discussion of each issue.

The four examples that follow illustrate how the board and administration can work effectively together as a team for the good of the overall school district. In particular, the issues show how the strategic and tactical roles, while different, can coordinate effectively, just as the various position players on a winning baseball team combine their differing functions and skills for the overall effectiveness of the team. A team brings different perspectives that can be melded in considering an issue so that aligned action results. But different perspectives can just as easily pull a team apart, making unified action impossible or guaranteeing that an action decided upon is flawed in terms of not addressing the needs of various roles. A team, then, isn't a team just because its members say it is one. Different perspectives are needed for people to become a team, though they alone won't guarantee that the individuals will become a team.

So what does make a team? Each player on a baseball team has different abilities and responsibilities, but all must work in an aligned way for the team to win. Similarly, the board has to meld the perspectives of its members to arrive at unified, final decisions that will benefit the school district. And once the board truly becomes a team internally, it must then become part of a larger school district team.

For the school district team, the board is like the pitcher. The team can't function on pitching alone, but neither can it function without it; the same holds true for the board's strategic expertise. Within the district, tactical and operational expertise are just as important and necessary as a catcher, infielders, and outfielders are to a baseball team. Parents, students, and other community members are also "players" to varying degrees. If the team on the baseball diamond is playing poorly, a chorus of boos will erupt from the stands; likewise, if staff, students, parents, and the community perceive the school system as faulty, a "chorus" of complaints and resistance will be heard and felt by the board.

Debates Over Class Size

Both parents and teachers usually desire smaller classes. However, debates about lower class size can quickly become intense and partisan. There's no definitive, research-based ideal class size, and smaller classes require more teachers and thus consume more resources. Debates over class size usually arise when a teachers union demands a "cap" during the collective bargaining process or when parents feel classes are too large compared to neighboring school districts or to what they feel their tax dollars should provide.

It's easy to argue that smaller classes have a variety of benefits without being harmful in any way to either teachers or students. But it's much harder to make a convincing case that student achievement will actually improve as a result of smaller classes or that they are worth the resources needed to bring them about. After all, boards must remember that there often are multiple claims on those resources, not all of which can be satisfied.

In promoting lower class sizes, teachers and parents aren't concerned with the need for allocating more resources—that's deemed to be "the board's problem"— they simply want tangible evidence of class-size relief.

The Strategic Perspective

For the board, the issue is whether or how to deploy existing resources given the political context. The more limited the available resources and the more politically charged the demand for smaller classrooms, the more difficult the issue becomes. On one hand, the board wants to be responsive to a change that is so intuitively and universally appealing. On the other, the cost of the additional personnel and physical space required is substantial, and there's little likelihood that expending these resources will significantly alter student achievement outcomes. So the question for a board immersed in this debate is often, "What's the affordable price in resources for political peace?"

Typically, the board won't want restrictive language on class sizes in teachers' contracts if it can avoid it; the board needs to account for future possible circumstances when resources might not be available to meet the contract provisions without taking those resources from a more pressing need. Equally important, the board doesn't want to be perceived as being on the wrong side of such an appealing initiative. However, the board must consider needs and options around long-term resource deployment at all levels of the entire school district. These are complex considerations that neither teachers nor parents are examining, and frankly, these future-focused concerns play weakly to the public when it has such a "right-now" issue that it's promoting. In short, the board will be forced to address the class-size issue more in the political terms of the teacher or parent demands than from an objective assessment of the right priorities in resource deployment.

The Tactical Perspective

This is a situation where the strategic and tactical perspectives are very similar. Administration needs to figure out the resource costs of lowering class sizes and the tradeoffs for shifting those costs. Those tradeoffs are of major concern to tacticians because they could undermine a number of other important school district initiatives that are either currently in place or soon will be.

Remember, an adjustment period is needed whenever a school district begins a new initiative, particularly by operational staff, whose natural tendency is to resist change. Therefore, among the tradeoffs administrators have to consider is teacher pushback. This holds true even for an issue like lower class sizes that teachers are promoting. Lowering class sizes will please teachers only if nothing else in their professional lives changes as a result. Yet tacticians know that available resources might require some tradeoffs, such as cutting noninstructional positions or cutting back on available teacher planning time. And when operational pushback occurs from teachers, administrators feel it far sooner and more intensively than the board. Consequently, it's crucial that administration thoroughly analyze these tradeoffs.

The Strategic-Tactical Blend

The board needs to know enough to take action on the demand for lower class sizes. If the board seriously wishes to consider lowering class sizes, it must first review a plan, crafted by the administration, on how the change will actually happen. Board members must understand what possible tradeoffs might be—information they can only obtain from the administration and to which they should give considerable weight.

If the board decides to oppose lowering class sizes, it likely will have to do two things:

1. *Compile credible and convincing data on the merits and drawbacks of lowering class sizes.* Because the board has neither the time nor the access needed to do the required research itself, it must charge the administration to do so.

2. *Share these data with the group demanding the class-size change.* This will lend the board more credibility.

This process will probably lead to the establishment of a new advisory committee. The committee will study class-size options in the context of both the research base and local school district issues, such as available space, budget implications, and short-term and long-term needs. The care and feeding of such a committee will be a significant new task for the administration, which also needs to ensure that the committee's outputs don't constrain the board's ultimate ability to make a decision. Given the time the administration will need to successfully perform this task, the board will have to authorize the administration to spend less time on some of its other responsibilities.

Three things become clear from this example:

1. The board, not the administration, must decide whether or not to lower class size. But the administrators, not the board, must craft the arguments for consideration, conduct the research, compile the evidence required, and coordinate the advisory committee study of this issue.

2. The board's decision likely will have much more to do with how to prioritize and allocate limited resources than it will with the merits of lowering class sizes. The board's commitment to strategic goals will be tested because the politically popular choice may be a bad choice for future resource commitments.

3. By directing administration to study a reduction of class size, the board has, wittingly or unwittingly, made this issue a strategic priority, whatever it ultimately decides. That's significant because the board should always be aware when and how its priorities have changed. In particular, if the board assigns considerable tactical resources to an issue, so that it becomes a new board priority, an existing priority or two will have to come off the table.

Negotiations With Teachers

Contract talks with teachers, typically done through some sort of collective bargaining process, are about taking one pot of resources and dividing control of the pot between two groups: the board and the collective bargaining unit, usually a teachers union. Whatever resources one group controls, the other group won't control.

Control over financial resources can be direct or indirect. *Direct control* refers to decisions about how much money will be spent and for what purposes, as well as decisions about salary schedules, benefits costs, and extra-duty pay. For example, if the teachers' contract says that each teacher will receive an annual 4% raise, then the board will lose control over a specific amount of resources and the teachers union will gain that control. The board will be contractually obligated to deliver on that monetary figure, no matter what the school district's fiscal circumstances are or might be in the future.

Indirect control refers to contract language that implies the need for certain sums without directly addressing specific expenditures. For example, consider a contractual guarantee of a certain class size. The class-size limits in the contract trigger the employment of additional teachers and teacher aides, as well as space accommodations when the contractual class-size limits are breached.

The natural dynamic between the board and a bargaining group is that both parties want as much control over as much of the resource pot as possible. However, the board rarely, if ever, gets to remove something from a contract because the political pushback usually is too great, unless the school district is in the midst of an intractable fiscal crisis. Practically, this means that whatever form of collaborative bargaining processes is used, a bargaining group will ask for as much as it can get and the board will give up as little as possible. That by definition makes for an adversarial rather than a collaborative bargaining relationship.

If the tone of bargaining becomes too adversarial, board members will make personal enemies out of the same operational staff that they need to foster ongoing improvement in the classroom. The school district's needs require that the two sides maintain at least a cordial and respectful relationship throughout the bargaining process. This tension between resource needs and role needs makes collective bargaining a very complicated process.

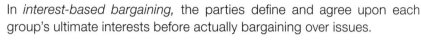

In *interest-based bargaining,* the parties define and agree upon each group's ultimate interests before actually bargaining over issues.

In *win-win bargaining,* the goal of bargaining is to have neither side "lose" to the other through making sure each side "wins" some things.

The Strategic Perspective

Why should board members sit at a bargaining table at all—why not just let the administration or the board's attorney handle things? After all, isn't collective bargaining a tactical responsibility that the board shouldn't micromanage? In this case, it's not; board members have to be at the bargaining table because the school district's resources are at issue, and only the board has the ultimate authority to decide who should control them.

Collective bargaining is one of those rare times when the board's strategic responsibilities directly interface with operational needs because of the overriding importance in determining resource control. From the board perspective, collective bargaining involves trying to say "no" in the most positive ways possible. That's a tricky position, but it becomes feasible if the board can get the bargaining group to understand all of the competing pulls for its resources. At the same time, the board must convince the group how important the staff is to the board and the entire school district. Typically, the bargaining group will demand tangible proof of the board's high regard in the form of staff control over additional resources. And thus the collective bargaining battle is joined.

You and other board members typically serve on a collective bargaining team and sit opposite of operational staff and, usually, the staff's professional bargaining representative. You'll have two disadvantages:

1. Unless your board has its own professional bargaining representative—usually, the board attorney—you won't know either the specifics of the contract or the school district's culture as well as the staff's bargaining representative will.

2. You and other board members don't typically interface directly with operational staff. This puts you and other board members at a disadvantage at the bargaining table.

Concerning the first disadvantage, board members who have backgrounds as negotiators or attorneys often assume that they can do the bargaining on behalf of the board and so save it some attorneys' fees. However, their negotiating skills are offset by their unfamiliarity with the school district's culture, as well as with state law that defines the limits of board authority on collective-bargaining issues, a highly technical legal area. This puts them at a "background disadvantage" compared to the staff bargaining representative sitting across the table. While this disadvantage might not be fatal to a skilled negotiator, it's an impediment for a board member in representing management at the bargaining table adequately, especially when he or she is representing the entire board and school district.

The second disadvantage is almost entirely role-based: It's highly unlikely the operational issues that teachers care passionately about will resonate as significantly for you as for them. Probably, many operational issues will seem comparably insignificant to you and even to tactical staff, and might strike you as requiring an unnecessary resource cost, especially in regard to other contract issues upon which you place more value. Different perspectives toward some bargaining issues can get in the way of maintaining positive, mutually respectful negotiations. As a result, board members at the negotiating table can lose respect for teachers—not a good outcome for anyone.

The Tactical Perspective

Administrators are more attuned to the needs for collective bargaining collaboration because they interact frequently with staff and will feel first the effects of any discontent about how the collective bargaining is going. Collective bargaining thus has the potential to make an administrator's life more difficult given any adverse reactions from teachers or other staff to the negotiations' processes and outcomes.

In addition, administrators are well-versed on the implications of contract language because they have to adhere to the contract daily and are most likely to be singled out if a staff member alleges that a contract violation has occurred. So administrators have very conservative interpretations of potential giveaways or tradeoffs in contracts. For example, teachers may want 10 more minutes of planning time per day (a giveaway by the board) and are willing to concede the board's request to take the special education coordinator out of the bargaining unit in exchange for this (a tradeoff). Administration knows that 10 more minutes per day of planning time for every teacher will greatly complicate scheduling and that it will also cost a lot of money to replace the teachers who are spending more time each day with children with new personnel. Giveaways and tradeoffs can make an administrator's professional life more difficult, particularly if they arise from contract language that limits the administrator's autonomy in dealing with operational staff.

Administrators want the board to maintain control over financial resources because they wish to maintain the contractual status quo as much as possible, given that administrators are responsible for correctly carrying out contract language. So, at the bargaining table, administrators are natural partners with the board—both represent management. In addition, administrators aren't typically part of employee bargaining groups, or, if they are, they're members of their own administrative group, apart from the employee group. An employee group won't represent administrators for any perceived contract violation, so administrators have no contractual loyalties to employee groups. They do have contractual loyalty to a board due to bridge responsibilities and their deeper personal familiarity with individual board members. Typically, they sit at the board table to assist and support board members in the collective bargaining process. There should never be doubt among any of the parties as to which side of a negotiating table administration sits.

The Strategic-Tactical Blend

Tacticians do the research and provide background materials for the board's bargaining team because they alone have intimate experience with application of the contract on a daily basis. Tacticians recommend contract changes and rationales for the board bargaining team's consideration and also offer historical perspective on how past contract language did or didn't work well for the school district.

Tacticians also suggest scenarios for possible bargaining points and offer perspective on how proposals from either side might play out. They might offer ongoing counsel on how to keep the tone of negotiations as positive as possible. But they do all of this at the direction and in support of the board's bargaining team and defer to what that team ultimately recommends for the full board's approval. While administrators can make suggestions as to bargaining strategies, tactics, or content, all the ultimate decisions belong to the board. In negotiations, as much as in anything, administrators are the board's strong right hand both at the bargaining table and between bargaining sessions.

Assessing Student Achievement

Everyone wants to assess the results of student achievement efforts. The community wants to know if its tax dollars are being well spent and looks at student achievement measures to determine whether they are. Parents want to know how their individual children are performing, usually in comparison to other children. Teachers want to know if what they are doing in the classroom is effective. School principals want to know how the entire school is doing and whether strengths or weaknesses are consistent across the entire school. School district administrators want to know what principals want to know, but across all schools, as well as how the organization compares to other school districts. Policymakers want to know how American students compare to students from other countries and what can be done on a wide-scale policy level to improve results.

A school board also wants to know how children in its school system are achieving because that's the litmus test for the success or failure of the school district's programs and expenditures. *A responsible school board shouldn't claim school district success, regardless of what other accomplishments it might have, if measures of student achievement aren't strong and improving.* But how a board determines the true level of student achievement isn't as simple as it might appear.

High-stakes state tests, such as those tied to the federal No Child Left Behind (NCLB) Act, receive enormous publicity and public comment. But these tests are only annual state-level assessments that don't assess the same learning across the nation and don't really capture what a child learns at a local level over the course of a full school year. Other standardized tests, such as the Iowa Tests of Basic Skills or the Stanford Achievement Test, look at student achievement across a large national base of students who have previously taken the test, producing a national norm of performance on the same learning. However, even though these test results can be accurately compared across states—although not to specific state standards as required by NCLB—they, too, are one-time events. In addition, no one can say with certainty that what a school is teaching links directly to what a nationally normed or a state-based exam is testing. Those who analyze test results might wonder whether students who didn't score well simply failed to learn what was presented or were never taught the material in the first place.

A student's grades give a specific look at student achievement at a classroom level and reflect what is actually being taught in the classroom. However, it's hard to accurately compare the grades of one teacher to those of another, much less to compare grades across schools and school districts. That's because most teachers use different criteria to determine a grade. For example, there's no way to tell if a B grade in one teacher's class might not mean the same as an A grade in another's class, or a C grade in still another's. Almost everyone has experienced either an "easy grader" or a "hard grader" in his or her school experience. In short, classroom grades can't be taken to mean that the same amount of learning took place in anything other than a single isolated classroom and, in some instances, not even then. That means that no single assessment measure will "do it all," though each assessment option has its strengths and weaknesses.

A fairly reasonable assessment of student achievement can be made by using combinations of all of these means, particularly if the assessment combination is tied to the data needs of specific school district roles—what achievement data the board, the administration, and the teachers want to see in order to inform their respective strategic, tactical, or operational activities.

The Strategic Perspective

The board's strategic responsibilities require it to determine how and where the school district can focus its energy and resources. The board has to use varied student data to identify patterns that indicate areas for improvement, areas that represent legitimate *strategic* targets for change.

The correct linkage between data and strategy is crucial. A lot of available data will be informative to other roles, but not to a strategic role. For example, an individual student's grades or state test scores—even those of a board member's own child—represent operational data, which is too personal and specific to qualify as strategic data.

To properly qualify as strategic, data have to show patterns of achievement across groups large enough to warrant a response by the full school district (for example, data that indicate a deficit in reading achievement across the entire school district). Data that show one school having achievement levels clearly below those of other schools might also warrant a response by the entire school district. The board would want to charge administration to investigate and address such a discrepancy based on the premise that all children in the organization deserve an equal opportunity to enjoy learning success. The board's strategic deployment of resources would be determined in part by the needs of students within individual schools, as measured by collective achievement results, and in part by a commitment to provide certain learning opportunities for all children in all schools.

However, the board shouldn't assume the same responsibility to address a classroom or even a grade-level deficit in one school. It doesn't need to do so because *the school will be looking at its own data and setting its own goals to catch such patterns and address such deficits itself.* The school's response, while not dictated by the board, still needs to align with the school district's overall strategic priorities.

The board might also look at data from the perspective of data breakouts, for example, by examining data about all male or all female students, all students who fall into a particular ethnic or socioeconomic group, or all students who receive special services. In each case, data patterns could result in the board setting a strategic charge to address student achievement issues within that school district subgroup.

The line between a board's strategic response and a school's internal needs can be summarized succinctly: Leave the school issues to the schools. School issues are reflected through grade-level and classroom-level data patterns; strategic issues are reflected through individual school or cross-school data patterns. School goals address school issues; district goals address districtwide issues.

The Tactical Perspective

The board wants to view achievement data as a means to identify school district goals and resource allocations for change. Administrators are also concerned with such decisions, if for no other reason than they have to carry out whatever board decisions are made based upon a data review. In addition, administrators need to consider how the data that go to the board are presented to the public. This can produce a dilemma because the purpose of the same data is different for a board than for the public.

As discussed in chapter 5, the board needs strategic data to make decisions about resource allocations, but it also might need to see tactical or even operational data—not to act upon it, but to provide context for better understanding of the strategic data. The public assesses the same data from the broadest possible perspective; the data either confirm that the school district is doing a good job or indicate that it's doing a poor job. For the board, data are diagnostic; they indicate what should be done next to improve the school district.

You can readily see how these different perspectives toward the same data can be troublesome, especially given open-meetings laws that require board information and actions to be transparent to the public. The board seeks student achievement and other data that aren't always "good news" to assess how the school district can improve. The board is interested in such data because it wants to make strategic decisions accordingly. But there's a danger that the public airing of such data will cause the public to lose confidence in the school district. Administration has to determine both how to present such data to the board and anticipate how the data presentation might strengthen rather than diminish the public's confidence in the school district.

Given the inherent limitations of the types of available achievement data, administration needs to make sure that both the achievement data a board sees and the interpretations a board makes from it are as accurate as possible. If those interpretations aren't accurate, then board charges will be based upon flawed premises, the plans tacticians devise won't accurately address student needs, and pushback from operational levels as a result will be stronger. In addition, subsequent changes needed to fix the faulty initial changes will be harder to implement because the operational staff's attitude will have hardened against any changes.

Administration knows that initiating change is hard and complicated work. It has to implement the right plan correctly the first time; it can't afford to start over with a different plan when the first plan crashes because of a misunderstanding of the data's essential meaning and significance.

This need for greater data accuracy is achieved through more data detail and more extensive analysis of the metrics, which take time to prepare and discuss. But a typically packed board agenda usually doesn't allow for much time for thorough data analysis. This means that the board generally has to rely upon tactical staff to undertake the data analysis and present it at the board's public meeting.

The Strategic-Tactical Blend

Data offer endless possibilities for detail and analysis. Clearly, the board and its administration need to agree on the focus and detail of the achievement data that the board will see. If the board doesn't provide initial direction to administration about what it wants to know (for example, "How are our low-income students achieving compared to the rest of our student population?" or "What are the three key areas where we should be celebrating success?"), then tacticians will substitute their own detail and priorities, which might not align with those of the board. When that happens, a data reanalysis is needed, time is lost, and frustrations on both sides mount.

It's essential that the board give direction about data analysis before administration begins this process. This might be difficult because the board doesn't know where the data will lead. Initially, then, the board should go with administration's analysis. The administration likely has been analyzing data for a while, and so has a good grasp of student achievement measures. Once the board has analyzed such data itself, it can give more specific direction the next time around; each subsequent time data are available, the board will become more focused and specific in its direction to administration. Past data analysis sharpens future hypotheses about data and requests.

How should such analyses be presented to the public? The answer isn't to try to explain each bit of data presented, but rather to demonstrate that the school district has adopted *a culture of rigorous data analysis,* preferably by using a district performance scorecard. When this is routinely done, the public will, over time, become acclimated to more complex levels of school district data, and such data will increase the public's confidence in the board and school district.

This process means administration will regularly present data at board meetings for discussion and analysis. If the board publicly presents its district goals, then the public will know the board is promoting continuous improvement, including a rigorous analysis of relevant data tied to those goals. This provides context for understanding board discussions around data in general and makes misunderstanding of any particular piece of data less likely.

This makes it critical that the board communicate its commitment to continuous school district improvement through ongoing public data analysis. The board will require a tactical plan for administration to craft and carry out. What guides administration in crafting such a plan are the school district's commitment to continuous improvement, a long-term strategic plan that provides an overall vision for the district, shorter-term goals that address particulars of the strategic plan, and ongoing analysis of data to determine whether the goals are being achieved. Such data analysis and presentations based on it should also identify the various constituent groups with whom the board should communicate and what messages and communication vehicles will be used. In short, assessment data become a means for diminishing public confusion and enhancing public confidence in the school district.

Strategic Budgeting

Resource allocation is about money (what is budgeted and spent) and time (how tactical and operational personnel use the hours available to them). Both types of resources should be aligned to the school district's goals and strategic plans. But in many districts, they aren't, leaving the organizations without a clear path by which to successfully carry out strategic charges. When it comes to budgeting, such an alignment is particularly important.

When a direct link exists between the school district's goals and its strategic plan, and how it spends its money, the allocation of resources is maximized for continuous improvement. If no such a link exists, then strategic initiatives must compete for resources that are going to other things—and those things might not even be on the board's radar screen. The result? Resources will become insufficient to meet strategic goals, and the district will be more limited in achieving continuous improvement.

The Strategic Perspective

Boards typically spend a lot of time worrying about the availability of sufficient funds, justifying to the public their use of money, and wondering whether they have enough political capital to ask for more funds via a referendum or other public request.

Typically, the board asks the community for more money when it can show that existing funds are running out, thus endangering current programs. The implied message—that the programs in place are valuable and shouldn't be lost—usually mobilizes the support of parents, who don't want their children to lose the opportunities being provided. But this argument might be a tougher sell to nonparent community members, who don't have a direct vested interest in those programs. This constituency cares more about results. It will ask such questions as:

- Are achievement scores good enough to maintain property values and keep community confidence in the school district strong?

- Will real estate values and local business interests be promoted by the school district's reputation as a strong system that draws people to the community?

- Will giving more money to a school district result in added value to the community?

Referenda rise or fall on such community-based assessments. The inherent weakness in this process is that school programs aren't as strongly linked to the perspective of the nonparent community as they could be. Since the community looks first to the district budget to assess whether the schools add value to the community, that budget and how it is developed can become essential to obtaining community support.

Because there generally is less money available than there are desires within the school district on how to spend it, the more aligned a budget is to a strategic plan and board goals, the more defensible the board's spending choices will be, both within and outside of the school district. But in most school districts, a budget isn't aligned in this fashion; rather, it's based on the previous budget.

This has two implications. The first is that budgets tend to gradually expand as short-term needs change and new costs are added to the budget to fund those new needs. Rarely is anything correspondingly dropped from the budget, and as a result, it continues to grow both vertically (more money needed to do the same things) and horizontally (more things to fund). In this sense, the budget itself drives the school district's priorities. Whatever is budgeted needs to be done, and whatever is to be done will have to be already in the budget or added to it.

When fiscal resources inevitably become scarce, painful budgetary bloodletting results. This sometimes is like the blood leeching of the Revolutionary War period, which was thought to draw "bad blood" from the system of an ill person, but instead had the effect of further weakening him or her. In a similar fashion, budgetary bloodletting forces a school district to reprioritize its budget quickly and from a crisis mentality, usually due to the failure of a referendum. School districts rarely make good short-term or long-term decisions under such pressure.

The second implication is that because priorities are driven by what is in the budget rather than the reverse—having the budget reflect those priorities—budgetary allocations are harder to defend because no strategic rationale exists for them. The board offers a weak argument when it goes to a well-informed and discerning public—or, more likely, a public that's fed up with continually paying higher and higher taxes—and requests more taxpayers' money to merely continue what has always been done. In a multimedia world where more information travels to more people faster, the board will find it increasingly difficult to say to the public, "Trust us to decide how much money we need and how much more you need to give us." Today, the board has to prove the need for more money and to clear a higher bar of public trust than ever before.

To the extent that the board can align its budgeting to its strategic plan and goals, credible proof becomes easier to obtain. After all, if the strategic plan really did emerge from a group that's representative of the community, and the board's goals are aligned to the strategic plan, there should be built-in community support for any budgetary expression of the strategic plan and goals.

To make the budget align to school district goals and the strategic plan, the board needs help from tactical staff. While the board's strategic responsibility is to align the budget to a school district's strategic priorities, administration's tactical responsibility is to determine how to actually do so.

The Tactical Perspective

Of course, changing budget priorities will immediately get administration's attention, not only because it will have to plan for such changes and their organizational ripple effects, but also because administrators are part of staff, and staff will surely be directly or indirectly affected by some of these changes. Administrators' own personal interests will cause them to give particular scrutiny to board budgetary decisions.

However, the administration's basic role is to create tactical plans by which to carry out board strategic charges. If the board's budgetary charges are strategic, any staff ripple effects will be within the context of moving toward a previously understood strategic direction. To the extent that this direction is tied to the school district's strategic plan, such decisions are contextually appropriate and will likely garner overall support.

But when the board's budgetary decisions aren't tied to a community-based vision, the likelihood of significant pushback increases. That presents a problem not only for the board but also, more immediately, for the administration. Tactical leaders will feel the brunt of the pushback from some of their administrative colleagues, operational staff, or both. The less aligned board budgetary priorities are and the more random they appear, the more pushback is likely from tactical and operational staffs, and the harder it will be to bring these priorities to fruition.

Covert pushback—a grudging acceptance of a new initiative without a corresponding commitment to making it a personal priority—can be just as damaging as overt pushback because it slows the implementation of the new initiative to a crawl. For successful organizational change to occur, each staff member has to feel enough commitment toward the new initiative to self-monitor the time and energy he or she puts into seeing the initiative through.

In responding to the board's budgetary decision, staff members find it easier to accept the continuation of old programs and policies, even if they're ineffective, than to embrace new ones, particularly if they eliminate some old initiatives. The administration knows this particular dynamic of the school culture well and will have to account for it in crafting an effective implementation plan. To the extent that the board's budget priorities adhere to a larger strategic vision, the administration's planning becomes that much easier and more successful in its implementation.

The Strategic-Tactical Blend

Administrators need to craft a budget for board review that clearly addresses the board's strategic priorities. This requires administrators to analyze each category of line items in the budget to determine how it either supports or is peripheral to the strategic plan and goals. During this process of mapping the budget to strategic priorities, administrators begin by looking at patterns of expenditures in terms of whether they directly support strategic priorities, indirectly do so (that is, while also supporting other things), or exclusively support other things.

Once this mapping is completed, the administration makes a report to the board about what the patterns signify. In doing so, administrators have to address a wide range of questions, including:

- Do the supporting expenditures predominate, or are they secondary in the budget?

- Are the budgetary categories or items that are aligned effective, or should more effective approaches be used?

- What budgetary categories or items don't align to strategic priorities? Do we need to continue to fund such things?

- Are categories or items that are indirectly aligned to the strategic plan and goals sufficiently aligned, or can they be better aligned?

As you might anticipate, considering budgetary priorities is no small task; there are complex considerations at play. For example, even if the school district's liability insurance isn't linked to a board goal, it might be viewed as a priority that requires funding because it's integral to the school district's wellbeing, no matter what strategic direction it takes. Another example: Budgetary funds for health insurance for staff or bus transportation for students are political necessities that extend beyond board goals and strategic priorities.

The board also needs to ask: If a large part of the budget is devoted to student instruction, how effective is that instruction? Is it responsible to spend resources for the right educational goals that don't result in effective applications to address those goals?

This task will take considerable time, and the administration can't complete it without some key feedback from operational staff. In all likelihood, some community interaction also will be required, particularly from parents, who have a strong vested interest in existing programs that impact their children.

Once completed, administrators' analysis and recommendations to the board provide a rich opportunity for thoughtful discussion and debate. In considering this research and recommendations, the board has to come to some conclusions on how the budget needs to be reprioritized. It won't be looking for a perfect alignment between its goals and all of the budget's line items—as mentioned, some organizational and political compromises inevitably have to be made to meet overall organizational needs. But to the extent that the board *can* make its budget more aligned with strategic priorities, this process will be productive.

By making a school district's budget an expression of strategic goals, rather than a diversion from or an impediment to their realization, the board moves toward budgetary alignment.

Chapter Summary

- A team is comprised of differing perspectives that align; its members work in a collaborative fashion to address common issues.

- The board must be both its own team and also a leading—but not dominant—member of a team of strategic, tactical, and organizational players within the school district.

Debates Over Class Size

- The board must decide whether the resources needed to lower class sizes will replace resources needed for its other priorities.

- The demands of constituents in a class-size debate tend toward the political and emotional, while the board tries to assess the issue objectively in terms of the school district's strategic interests. This often makes for an unproductive debate.

- Lower class sizes threaten to take away resources from existing programs and might force undesirable operational tradeoffs.

- The board must make the final decision about class sizes, while the administration compiles and sorts through the information that will serve as the basis for that decision.

Negotiations With Teachers

- There's a tension at the bargaining table between the board's resource needs (competition between the board and teachers for control of the same resources) and its role needs (the desirability of maintaining cordiality and respect between board members and those who are working to continually improve the classroom environment).

- A board goal is to say "no" in as kind and positive a way as possible.

- A bargaining group expects tangible (contractual) proof of the board's high regard for its members.

- Board members at the bargaining table have two immediate disadvantages: (1) They're unfamiliar with the contract and the accompanying staff culture, and (2) they have a natural, role-based lack of understanding for many operational concerns.

- The board must be directly represented at the negotiating table because determining who controls school district resources is a fundamental strategic responsibility.

- Administrators, being tacticians, are natural allies to the board at the bargaining table.

- Administrators, not board members, conduct the research and prepare the bargaining positions that board members will advocate.

Assessing Student Achievement

- No single data source will tell a board all it wants to know.

- Good strategic data must accurately represent what a board wants to know yet still focus the board toward appropriate strategic responses that represent the school district.

- Strategically, the board's full organizational response should encompass decisions ranging from school district needs to individual school needs to school district subgroup needs.

- Decisions about issues within a school should be left to that school, not the board, as long as the school's decisions are within the parameters of the district's strategic priorities.

- Tacticians are concerned that the same data used diagnostically by a board can be used for evaluative purposes by the public, especially when such data are presented at a public board meeting.

- A board and its administration need to collaboratively determine how data analysis is to be done and what conclusions from the analysis should be drawn.

- The more frequently data are publicly analyzed and discussed by the board, the more familiar and comfortable the public will become with the culture of rigorous data analysis that the board has established.

Strategic Budgeting

- At every level of the school district, money and time commitments should be aligned to strategic priorities.

- By aligning the budget to strategic priorities, the board makes spending more efficient and focused than by allowing the budget itself to define priorities by default.

- A budget aligned to strategic priorities is more defendable to the public.

- The board determines that the budget should be aligned to strategic priorities, administrators craft a plan that does so, and the board then approves that plan.

- Tacticians worry about how to defend the board's budgetary decisions from operational overt or covert pushback.

- Tacticians need to "map" a budget to determine what's directly aligned to strategic priorities, what's indirectly aligned, and what isn't aligned, and they need to obtain feedback from operational staff on their findings, before they can make recommendations to the board.

- The board shouldn't as much strive to perfectly align a budget to strategic priorities as to cause the budget to support strategic priorities rather than compete with them.

7

The Ethics of Board Service

If only the board can assume a strategic role, why do so many board members abandon that role and venture into a tactical role? Table 7-1 summarizes the reasons we've discussed. But once you understand your board role as part of a complex, collaborative system, you'll see the true value and power of your strategic role for making a poor school district into a good one and a good one into a great one.

Once you accept your role as a member of the school district *team*, you'll be free to devote your time and energy to the one thing that only you and other board members can do successfully: to assume strategic leadership and demonstrate that leadership through developing strategic charges. And once you accept both the potential and the limits of the strategic role, you'll become essential to any improvement effort by the school district and highly desirable as both a leader and as a symbol of aligned, sustained, and effective school district change.

Table 7-1: Why Many Board Members Abandon Their Strategic Role

Experience	It's so tempting to take what you know from your personal life and try to apply it to school districts as if there were no need for any translation.
Action Rather Than Leadership	The strategic role, though powerful, is indirect. Many people connect leadership with *doing* (making plans oneself) rather than *leading* (setting the direction but allowing others to carry out the direction).
Personal Agenda	Board members come to a board because of tactical or operational issues they understand through the experiences of their own or a close friend's children.
Overestimation of Tactical Effects	Board members think their tactics will change the school district, but those tactics inevitably fail to account for operational realities and needs.
More Fun	It's just plain more fun to dabble into tactics than it is to stick to strategies.
Time Concerns	Of all the role groups, boards are most in a hurry to see change occur. These board members think that by taking over tactics themselves, change will speed up.

However, here's the rub: No one can make a board member assume the strategic role. True, at every board election, a board member is held accountable for what he or she did the preceding term. But on a day-to-day basis, he or she is evaluated by no one, and no one can veto a board's decisions. At best, a superintendent can advise and try to convince, but he or she can't dictate strategic policy. And as soon as the board-superintendent relationship heads south, so does the superintendent, while the school board remains. For this reason, a superintendent will only go so far in trying to redirect a board member who has gone astray. And the board president, along with a board majority, can try to manage out-of-role members, but this will only slow the board bleeding—not stop it—if the board members at issue don't agree to change their behaviors. *The most effective policing of a board member's behavior will come from himself or herself.*

The plain fact of the matter is that a board member's multiyear term is a period during which he or she can either add value or wreak havoc, whether knowingly or unknowingly. Yet no one is going to police a board member's behaviors as effectively as the individual member himself or herself. So a successful board member must make a personal commitment to buying into a strategic leadership role. To add value, he or she should understand and try to live the ethics of the strategic role, including:

- Committing to the discipline of collaboration

- Staying within your strategic role

- Being aware of slipping into micromanaging behaviors

- Crafting communications so that individuals within and outside the school system will understand what the board wants to communicate

- Worrying as much about how change will affect the players in the school system as about the nature of the change itself

- Modeling thoughtful and aligned behaviors

- Responding humanely to problems with students and staff while also setting challenging but attainable targets for school district improvement

This constitutes the ethics of a strategic role. There are no rules or laws that govern a board member's behavior; there's nothing anyone else can effectively enforce. There's only each board member's ethical commitment to embrace a strategic role as the most effective way to move the school district forward, even if it isn't the most personally interesting or rewarding role to embrace. In short, a board member must buy into a *team* concept and embrace a strategic *team* role.

Collaborating for Change

Collaboration isn't just a style that you can choose or not because being a successful school board member is due to your talent and skill sets alone. It isn't. *Rather, collaboration is essential to your role; you and other board members must work collaboratively to make real change in the school district happen.*

So if collaboration is essential to a board member's success, what are the rules for successful collaboration?

1. Craft strategic charges with input from the larger community.

2. Assign the planning to achieve these charges to tactical staff.

3. Assess, through reliable data, progress toward attaining those strategic charges.

4. Highlight school district achievements and opportunities for improvement.

A board that consistently follows these four rules provides tremendous strategic leadership to the school district that will enable it to achieve ever greater things in the future.

In short, the functional definition of collaboration for a school board is: Stay strategic and don't get tactical or operational; work with others and don't make any of your decisions in isolation from other roles and groups; be aware of different needs and how they affect others' perceptions of time and their communications; don't assume others will understand your intent through your board actions alone; and be the visionary that every great school system must have.

Above all, be a collaborative team member both with your fellow board members and with people in other roles. Believe in the power and expertise of your strategic role, but respect the expertise and necessity of tactical and operational roles. Provide the strategic guidance that only the school board can. Be the visionary dreamer that every great school system must have.

Is it really this simple? Yes, it really is.

But being a collaborative board member isn't easy. It's tremendously time-consuming, sometimes frustrating, and always challenging. You need to realize that your ideas for change typically won't become school district realities in the precise way that you conceived them. If they survive at all, they'll be molded by tactical and operational realities, as well as by political, legal, and socioeconomic realities from outside the school district. "Your" idea will become everyone's idea, and your ego will probably be bruised in the process. But your visionary dreams will ultimately be realized, one step at a time.

Achieving the Gold Standard

Many school districts aren't yet good, and most of those that are—or think they are— aren't yet great. But all of them have the potential to become great. That's the gold-standard promise that is ushering us into one of the most exciting and potentially revolutionary times in the history of public education.

Yet at least four long-term developments are putting increased strain on the educational field:

1. Internet technology, making for more sophisticated and accessible data

2. Groundbreaking scientific research on the brain and on how we learn, leading to improved learning strategies and techniques

3. Technologically driven communications vehicles, encouraging more and faster organizational transparency

4. The workforce demands of a global economy, resulting in more people being needed who not only can master facts and concepts, but also can analyze and synthesize them

These developments require a more sophisticated approach than ever before to school district leadership, particularly at the board level. No longer can a school board be content with ensuring that the school district keeps running smoothly, teacher contracts are obtained with a minimum of discontent, and the community is happy enough with its schools to pass an occasional referendum. While these used to be a sterling trio of accomplishments for any school board, they represent barely adequate performance today. The future is making more frequent and complex demands upon public schools; those demands bang ever harder and more impatiently on every schoolhouse door.

As demands for schools to transform themselves become ever more strident, a school's leadership must transform itself as well to stay current with and to stay ahead of the demands. This need for the transformation of school leadership, particularly board leadership, is the impetus of this book.

For a school board, *the gold standard for board leadership comes from leading from a strategic role through a collaborative approach so as to provide the visionary leadership that will turn a system of schools into an aligned school system.* This kind of leadership is within the grasp of every citizen who aspires to serve on a school board.

Everyone is qualified to fulfill this role. Your leadership roadmap is before you, and it's simple to read. You just need to understand how a complex school system works and make a commitment to serving collaboratively from within the framework of a strategic role. All the time, effort, challenge, messiness, and frustration inherent in serving in one of the most important public-service positions will also bring you immense satisfaction and benefit the school district.

A board of education needs to formally and annually reflect upon its effectiveness. Boards can reflect on the school district's mission, vision, values, and goals; progress in achieving the goals of their strategic plan; their effectiveness as a team; and the quality of their communication with tactical and operational staffs and with the public. We've designed Table 7-2 (page 128), which is grounded in research and best practice, to serve as a checkpoint for boards to apply the tools, strategies, and principles we've outlined in this book.

The appendix *A Rubric for Achieving the Gold Standard* (page 148) contains a longer version of this table. With either form, you can assess your board's performance and determine where you need to go to reach a gold standard of board function and leadership.

Two concluding observations on the gold standard: First, while this rubric is primarily designed for board members, it can also be used by tactical and operational leaders. We've emphasized throughout this book the importance of strategic leaders working collaboratively with their tactical and operational counterparts to achieve the gold standard. No board, whatever its effort, will ever alone attain the gold standard independent of staff expertise at the tactical and operational levels.

Second, the notion of a board's strategic role in creating an effective school system is relatively new, even if the desire for an effective school system is not. Some of the concepts and practices we've discussed, such as the district performance scorecard, will continue to be developed and refined. While we've attempted to chart a clear path for the strategic role, the practices that derive from that role are still evolving.

Now It's Up to You

Many school districts are hungry for visionary and effective leadership that leads to an aligned, continually improving school district. Such leadership is now within your reach. You've only to grasp it—lightly and with an eye toward collaboration—to transform both your contributions as a board member and the leadership of your whole board. With such leadership, you can help make learning potent and successful for all children. Such a visionary role for school board leadership excellence is yours for the taking. Seize it now.

Table 7-2: A Rubric for the Gold Standard

	Is Confused About the Strategic Role 1	Understands the Strategic Role 2	Fulfills the Strategic Role 3
Setting mission, vision, values, and goals	The board lacks an articulated, strategic vision and direction, and focused goals to guide work.	The board sets an articulated strategic vision and direction that result in clear, precise, and focused goals by which to guide the school district's work.	The board works collaboratively by utilizing extensive stakeholder input to set clear, precise, and focused organizational goals that are aligned to strategic priorities that guide the district's work.
Building a collaborative culture through shared leadership	The board addresses random acts of improvement. The lack of collaboration and trust among the strategic, tactical, and operational roles results in independent "silos" of unaligned efforts.	The board is committed to continuous improvement by the school district. It recognizes that collaboration and mutual trust among the three roles are necessary to form a sustained partnership.	The board creates a culture that embraces ongoing change and continuous improvement. It works collaboratively with the other two roles so that all three form a partnership based on mutual trust.
Measuring the important things to engage in data-driven decision-making	The board has insufficient data to guide its strategic priorities. It doesn't use a district performance scorecard to identify what its priorities are and to monitor progress in achieving goals; it has a scorecard but doesn't use it, or uses it to micromanage.	The board systematically uses data to focus upon its strategic priorities. It utilizes a scorecard to identify and track indicators of key strategic priorities, but doesn't use the scorecard to report progress to the community.	The board systematically uses student, classwide, and schoolwide data to focus on its strategic priorities. It also utilizes a scorecard to identify and track key strategic priority indicators and as a way of reporting progress toward meeting goals to the community.
Aligning roles, responsibilities, and behaviors with goals and actions	The board doesn't stay within its strategic role, but instead meddles in other roles' responsibilities.	The board adheres to its strategic role and recognizes the different levels of role expertise within the school district.	Board members consistently self-monitor to stay within the strategic role. They encourage collaborative efforts that tap the expertise found at each role.

	Is Confused About the Strategic Role 1	Understands the Strategic Role 2	Fulfills the Strategic Role 3
Building system accountability at all levels	The board has insufficient data to be accountable to the community for organizational progress. It either doesn't have the right data or doesn't know how to appropriately analyze data to guide continuous improvement.	The board has the data it needs to make strategic decisions that will lead to school system progress and to be accountable to the community. The board uses accurate, reliable, and appropriate data for strategic decision-making, and through this data, ensures its accountability to the community for continuous improvement.	Board members know how to appropriately analyze data to guide continuous improvement.
Evaluating the organization's, not an individual's, performance	The board confuses the evaluation of individual performance with the monitoring of organizational performance.	The board knows the difference between monitoring (oversight of process) and evaluating (determining overall effectiveness through outcomes) organizational performance.	The board monitors *organizational* performance, while allowing the evaluation of individual performance to take place at the tactical and operational levels.
Communicating with all stakeholders	The board doesn't recognize that different constituencies require different communication strategies. At its public meetings, the board doesn't have time to discuss the scorecard. Agenda issues for public discussion aren't aligned to strategic priorities.	The board recognizes that communicating with other roles and audiences is more complex than only communicating internally. The board regularly uses its scorecard to publicly focus upon its strategic priorities.	The board uses a variety of strategies to communicate appropriately with different roles and other constituencies. It uses its scorecard at each public meeting to focus upon its strategic priorities and to demonstrate results.
Assessing stakeholder perceptions	The board doesn't use stakeholder satisfaction data, fails to use what it collects, or uses them in isolation and makes inappropriate decisions. The board acts on an individual need without validating whether it's representative of a community need.	The board understands that it shouldn't act on the basis of an individual's needs alone and uses perception surveys to identify stakeholder desires.	The board links perception data with other indicators of success to determine long-term and short-term priorities.

Appendices

Visit **go.solution-tree.com/schoolboards**
to download these reproducibles.

Communication Structures and Processes

Strategic to Tactical and Operational	Tactical to Operational and Strategic	Operational to Tactical and Strategic
Communication boards	Employee forums	Action plan findings
Other progress reports	Employee key communications	Satisfaction data
District leadership team two-way communication: listening and responding	School leadership teams' two-way communication: listening and responding	Feedback from grade-level and department teams
Board committees	District, grade-level, and department committees	Vertical team articulation
Strategic plan: mission, vision, values, and goals	School improvement plan: mission, vision, values, and goals	Grade-level and team improvement targets
District office performance: aligning goals	Building leadership performance: aligning goals	Staff performance: aligning goals
Electronic communication: district website	Electronic communication: school website	Electronic communication: website internal tools and information
District performance scorecard	School performance scorecard	Classroom, grade-level, and department communication boards
		Student data folders

Collaborative Leadership Structures

Grade-Level and Department Teams	School Leadership Team	District, Program, and Division Teams or Committees	District Leadership Team
The grade-level and department teams meet weekly to address the four critical questions of a professional learning community (DuFour, DuFour, Eaker, & Many, 2006):	The school leadership team meets twice monthly or as needed to address four purposes:	The district program, division teams, and district committees meet monthly or as needed to address these purposes:	The district leadership team meets quarterly, or as needed, to address these four purposes:
1. What should students know and be able to do? (curriculum)	1. Understand expectations and needs of school stakeholders.	• Develop systematic tools, strategies, and skills to address what everyone within the system is required to do well.	1. Understand expectations and needs of district stakeholders.
2. How will we know if they are learning? (assessment)	2. Respond to learned expectations and needs.	• Consider ROI (Return On Investment) to be certain that the results of pilot studies add value before they are deployed systemwide.	2. Respond to expectations and needs that emerged through the work of the other teams.
3. What will we do if they aren't? (instruction and intervention)	3. Set school direction through goals, measures, and action plans.	They receive a specific charge based on expectations, needs, and requirements that have been identified by school and district leadership teams, the board, superintendent, or union association.	3. Set district direction through goals, measures, and action plans.
4. What will we do if they are? (instruction and enrichment)	4. Monitor school results and act on data to ensure improvement.	There may be standing or temporary assignments to these committees.	4. Monitor district results and act on data to ensure improvement.
Grade-level and department team planning time is essential.	Team members must be skilled at using collaborative tools, strategies, and skills for efficient work.		Team members must be skilled with collaborative tools, strategies, and skills for efficient and effective work.
Team members must be skilled with collaborative tools, strategies, and skills for efficient and effective work.	A member of the team serves as a representative to the district leadership team to ensure two-way communication.		Membership is rotational, usually with a 2-year term.
A member of the team or department serves as a representative to the school leadership team to ensure two-way communication.	Membership is rotational, with members usually serving a 2-year term.		Stakeholder groups include the board, parents, certified staff, noncertified staff, administration, and union and staff associations.

Rick Stiggins' EDGE Analysis of Assessment System Users and Uses

Implications for the Assessment System   **Goal:** Student Achievement   **Indicator:** Illinois Standards Achievement Test

	Student	Classroom	Grade-Level and Department Team	School	Program	District
Implications for the Assessment System	What decisions about their learning will students need to make?	What decisions will classroom teachers need to make?	What decisions will grade-level and departmental teams need to make?	What decisions will the school need to make?	What decisions will district program or departments need to make?	What decisions will the district need to make?
	What information do they need to make those decisions?	What information do they need to make those decisions?	What information do they need to make those decisions?	What information does it need to make those decisions?	What information do they need to make those decisions?	What information does it need to make those decisions?
	What are the implications for the assessment system?	What are the implications for the assessment system?	What are the implications for the assessment system?	What are the implications for the assessment system?	What are the implications for the assessment system?	What are the implications for the assessment system?
Goal: Student Achievement	What am I supposed to know and be able to do?	What are my students supposed to know and be able to do?	What are the benchmarks for each grade level or department we need to meet?	What is the state standard to be met?	What are our goals for meeting the state standard?	What is the state standard to be met?
Indicator: Illinois Standards Achievement Test	What have I learned already, and what do I still need to work on?	What have they learned already, and what do they still need to work on?	What percent of all students in the grade level and department are meeting, and what percent aren't meeting, the benchmarks, disaggregated by subgroup populations?	What percent of students in the school are exceeding, meeting, not meeting, or in academic warning related to the standard?	What percent of students—disaggregated by subgroup population across the district and or by schools—are exceeding, meeting, not meeting, or in academic warning related to each goal of the standard?	What percent of all district students are exceeding, meeting, not meeting, or in academic warning related to the standard?

continued on next page →

The School Board Fieldbook © 2009 Solution Tree Press • www.solution-tree.com
Visit **go.solution-tree.com/schoolboards** to download this page.

Student	Classroom	Grade-Level and Department Team	School	Program	District
Did I show growth over the prior year related to each goal of the standard?	Which students showed growth over the prior year related to each goal of the standard?	What percent of all students in the grade level and department showed growth over the prior year related to each goal of the standard by subgroup population?	What percent of students in the school showed growth over the prior year related to the standard?	What percent of students in the district showed academic growth over the prior year related to each goal of the standard, disaggregated by subgroup populations across the district and/or by schools?	What percent of all students in the district showed growth over the prior year related to the standard?
Have I met the state achievement expectations?	Have they met the state achievement expectations?	Did a sufficient number of students in the grade level or department meet or exceed the district's target for meeting state or NCLB requirements?	Did the targeted number of students in the school meet or exceed the standard this year to meet state and NCLB requirements?	Did the targeted number of students in the district by subgroup population meet or exceed each goal of the standard this year to meet the state and NCLB requirements?	Did the targeted number of students in the district meet or exceed the standard this year to meet the state and NCLB requirements?
			How does the percent of students in the school meeting or exceeding the standard this year compare with benchmark schools?	How does the percent of students meeting or exceeding each goal of the state standard compare with benchmark districts?	How does the percent of students in the district who meet or exceed the standard this year compare with benchmark districts?

Adapted from Stiggins, R. (2006, November–December). Assessment FOR learning: A key to motivation and achievement. *Phi Delta Kappan EDge, 2*(2), 1–20.

Classroom Communication Boards

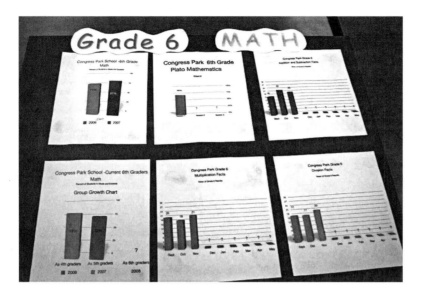

This classroom communication board allows the sixth-grade team at an elementary school to see data and metrics aligned to school and district improvement goals. Some data show how a group of sixth-grade students did in the fourth and fifth grades so that their educational growth can be studied. The board translates goals into grade-level metrics and targets that guide the team's action plans. In this way, the communication board gives meaning to the work that team members do.

The sixth-grade team frequently monitors students' progress to address refinements in actions and progress in results. Key sources of data include state summative test results; district formative benchmark test results; and classroom and short-cycle assessment aligned to the district benchmarks and state standards. Unless data can be communicated clearly at each role level, teachers in particular probably won't see how their work connects to school and district goals. Communication boards provide a visual way to communicate progress at each level and to create a data picture to show results to others.

The School Board Fieldbook © 2009 Solution Tree Press • www.solution-tree.com
Visit **go.solution-tree.com/schoolboards** to download this page.

Satisfaction Survey Alignment

Satisfaction Survey Items

It's important that satisfaction survey items align with the school district's mission, vision, values, and goals. No question should be placed on a survey for which the organization is unwilling to change actions or to address behaviors. It's better to have no satisfaction data than to have them and not report and respond to them as soon as is practically possible. It's important to include perception data in the district performance scorecard because they reveal how stakeholders feel about programs and services being provided.

Questions should also align across stakeholder groups, though their wording can vary according to the "language" of the particular group to whom the questions are addressed.

Surveys are administered annually and administered at a place and time when at least 95% of all stakeholders can complete them. They are offered electronically to respondents and scored, graphed, and reported within 10 days after the collection of data is completed. Questions address particular issues, roles, and responsibilities, not the performance of individual staff members. The following example is derived from a school district's mission, vision, and goals.

Student	Parent	Staff
1. I know the essential curriculum skills I'm expected to learn in order to be successful at the next grade level. 2. I know how I'm progressing in achieving those essential curriculum skills. 3. I know how my teacher feels I'm progressing in achieving those essential curriculum skills. 4. I take responsibility to record my results and compare them to the expectations set for my grade level. 5. My data show that I'm improving.	1. I'm aware of the essential curriculum skills my child needs to learn this school year. 2. I know how my child is progressing in achieving those essential curriculum skills. 3. I'm adequately informed throughout the year about my child's progress. 4. I'm aware of the school's improvement goals for the current school year. 5. I know how my school is progressing in achieving its improvement goals.	1. I teach the essential curriculum skills my students are expected to learn. 2. I know how each child is progressing in achieving those essential curriculum skills. 3. I assist students and parents in taking responsibility for setting and tracking goals to show growth and improvement. 4. I work with my grade-level and department team to improve results aligned to school and district improvement goals. 5. I know how my school and district are progressing in achieving their improvement goals.

Alignment Framework

Strategic to Tactical and Operational

Alignment Framework	Key Strategic Questions for School District and Individual Schools	Strategic Tools and Strategies	Key Questions for Tactical (Administrative), Operational (Teaching) Staff, Teams, Classrooms, and Students	Tactical and Operational Tools
Mission	What are our top priorities?	Strategic or improvement priorities	What are the essential standards and benchmarks all students should know and be able to do?	Essential learning targets Subgroup targets
Vision	Where do we want to be?	Strategic or improvement plan	What knowledge, skills, and processes do students need to be successful lifelong learners?	Subject-area criteria for excellence
Values	What beliefs and commitments do we share that will guide our work?	Strategic core beliefs, values, and parameters	What ground rules and commitments should guide our actions and behaviors?	Classroom ground rules Classroom commitments School rules
Needs Assessment	Where are we now?	Strategic key indicators Summative and baseline assessment data Gap analysis	What do we know? What do we need to know?	Preassessment data Assessment for diagnostic purposes (before teaching commences) Assessment for evaluative purposes (after teaching is completed) Gap analysis

continued on next page ↓

Alignment Framework	Key Strategic Questions for School District and Individual Schools	Strategic Tools and Strategies	Key Questions for Tactical (Administrative), Operational (Teaching) Staff, Teams, Classrooms, and Students	Tactical and Operational Tools
Goals: Action Plans	How do we get from where we are to where we need to be?	District goals and related action plans tied to targets Research best practices High-leverage strategies	How do you get from where you are to where you need to be?	SMART goals Lesson plan Class goal plans Student goal plans Targeted staff development Team goals and school goals
Results	What are we learning? Are we making progress?	Ongoing assessment and benchmarking Monitoring and reporting strategies Learning goal target, instructional steps, and timeline to reach learning goal target District performance scorecard Celebrations of successes ("wins")	What do we do when results show we haven't learned? What do we do when results show we have learned?	Ongoing formative assessment Feedback on what has or hasn't been learned Differentiated instruction Interventions—enrichment and remediation Celebrations

Strategic Plan Flowchart

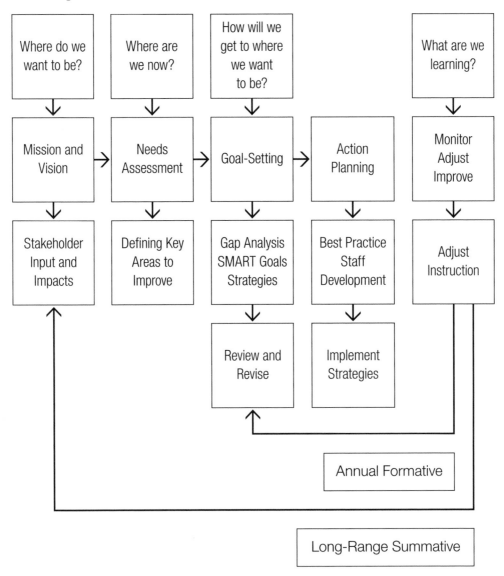

Adapted from Jan O'Neill and Anne Conzemius, *The Power of SMART Goals: Using Goals to Improve Student Learning* (2006, Solution Tree). Used with permission.

Scorecard Metrics

Metric Examples	Explanation
For each metric on the scorecard, the board must be clear about what it indicates and how to interpret it. A challenge for the board is to be certain that the right metric has been selected. The metric is an indicator by which progress can be tracked and reported. Backup data provide the board with information that tactical and operational employees use to find root causes for scorecard indicator results and address action plans to improve results.	
ISAT Reading & math grades 3–8 Current reading & math metrics 74/88	The current scores indicate that 74% of all students tested on the Illinois state reading standards test in grades 3–8 met or exceeded reading standards, while 88% of all students tested on the state mathematics test in grades 3–8 met or exceeded math standards.
Staff satisfaction surveys Current staff satisfaction 82/79/77	The current scores indicate that 82% of elementary, 79% of middle, and 77% of high school staff members surveyed represent composite "agree" or "strongly agree" responses to all questions on the survey.
State Annual Financial Profile Current 4.0	If a district receives a score of 3.54–4.00, it's in the highest category of *financial recognition.* These districts require little or no oversight or intervention by the state unless requested by the district.
Student Discipline Current 23/31	The current scores indicate that 23 students at the middle schools and 31 students at the high schools received more than two Level 2 or Level 3 discipline referrals.

District Performance Scorecard

continued on next page →

Priority/Aim	Indicators	When	B	G/T	C	Measure
Student Achievement Annually improve student performance in literacy and numeracy.	ISEL K–2	Annually	83	88	84	ISEL: % students meet/exceed standard ISAT: % students meet/exceed standard ACT: % students scoring higher than state average GradRate: % students entering 9th grade who graduate in 4 years NWEA: % students meet growth targets Local Benchmarks: % students meet/exceed grade level benchmarks Achievement Benchmarks: Rank of District ISAT results compared to all districts in the county in the areas of reading, math, and science
	ISAT Reading/Math 3–8	Annually	73/82	78/87	74/88	
	ACT 11	Annually	60	66	60	
	GRADUATION RATE	Annually	77	83	80	
	NWEA Reading/Math Growth 3–7	2x Year	45/49	55/58	48/52	
	Local Benchmarks Elem K–5/ 6–8	Trimester	66/55	72/65	73/63	
	Local Benchmarks High 9–12	Semester	53	60	55	
	Achieve. Benchmarks Read	Annually	4/12	2/12	4/12	
	Achieve. Benchmarks Math	Annually	3/12	2/12	2/12	
	Achieve. Benchmarks Sci	Annually	3/12	2/12	2/12	

continued on next page →

Priority/Aim	Indicators	When	B	G/T	C	Measure
Safe & Nurturing Environment Continuously provide a safe and nurturing climate.	Discipline Suspen./Expul.: Middle/High	Annually	.69/.93	1%/1%	.73/1.4	Discipline Susp.: State Discipline Report
	Disc. Class 2–3 Referrals: Middle/High	Monthly	27/39	20/25	23/31	Discipline Class Level 2/3 Referrals: Number
	Class Size PK–2/3–5/6–12	2x Year	23/25/27	23/25/27	22/25/28	Class Size: Class Size Average compared to guidelines
	Organ. Health Elem/Middle/High	Annually	63/57/51	75/75/75	70/65/59	Organ. Health: Composite Organ. Health Survey Results
	Facility Assessment Elem/Mid/High	Quarterly	78/71/65	80/80/80	75/77/68	Facility Assess: Comp Results % Agree/Strongly Agree
	Facility Usage Elem/Middle/High	Annually	98/95/90	95/95/95	100/95/93	Facility Usage: % Space Utilization
Fiscal Health Annually maintain highest "recognition" status on the state financial profile.	State Annual Financial Report	Annually	3.5	4.0	4.0	Annual Financial Report: State rating
	Audit	Annually	None	None	None	Audit: Audit report findings
	3 Year Projection (Ed Fund)	Annually	43	30	51	Ed Fund 3 Yr Projection: % Fund Balance
	3 Year Projection (Combined)	Annually	45.5	30	53	Combined 3 Yr Projection: % Fund Balance
	Budget to Actual (Ed Fund)	Quarterly	103/99	+/- 2%	103/98	Ed Fund: Forecast to Budget Variance % Rev to Expend
	Budget to Actual (Combined)	Quarterly	103/98	+/- 2%	103/97	Combined:: Forecast to Budget Variance % Rev to Expend

Priority/Aim	Indicators	When	B	G/T	C	Measure
Customer Service Continuously improve satisfaction with students, parents, and community.	Student Satisfaction Elem/Middle/High	Annually	86/77/75	85/85/85	88/81/80	Student Sat. Survey: Composite % Agree/Strongly Agree
	Parent Satisfaction Elem/Middle/High	Annually	88/81/75	85/85/85	85/80/81	Parent Sat. Survey: Composite % Agree/Strongly Agree
	Community Satisfaction	Bi-Yearly	83	85	83	Com. Sat. Survey: Composite % Agree/Strongly Agree
Quality Personnel Annually attract and retain quality personnel.	Staff Satisfaction Elem/Middle/High	Annually	79/71/67	85/85/85	82/79/77	Staff Sat. Survey: Composite % Agree/Strongly Agree
	Board Certified Elem/Middle/High	Annually	8/5/12	20/20/20	10/7/15	Board Certified Teachers: % Board Certified Teachers
	Retention Elem/Middle/High	Annually	85/81/80	90/85/85	88/82/78	Retention: Average Retention Rate of certified staff compared to prior year excluding retirements

The School Board Fieldbook © 2009 Solution Tree Press • www.solution-tree.com
Visit **go.solution-tree.com/schoolboards** to download this page.

Scorecard Backup Data

Measurement Example	Examples of Backup Data
ISAT reading and math grades 3–8 PSAE (ACT) grade 11 % met state standards % exceeded state standards	Individual district grade-level scores Individual district grade-level scores in four categories: exceeds, meets, doesn't meet, and academic warning Individual district grade-level scores, disaggregated by student subgroup in the four categories stated earlier Individual grade-level scores by school, disaggregated by student subgroup in the four categories Trend data
Staff satisfaction surveys % Agree % Strongly Agree Note: Survey questions are aligned to the district's mission, vision, and strategic objectives and goals.	District, grade-level, and department scores Elementary, middle, and high school scores Individual, grade-level, and department scores by school District scores broken out by gender Questions with more than 5% No Opinion or Neutral Questions with more than 33% Strongly Disagree or Disagree Questions with more than 10% Agree Trend data
State annual financial profile State rating	Fund balance to revenue ratio Expenditure to revenue ratio Number of days cash on hand Percent of short-term borrowing ability remaining Percent of long-term debt margin remaining Comparative data to similar and high-performing districts Trend data
Student Discipline Level 2 and 3: Number of discipline referrals per grade-level section	Number of students in middle school with more than two Level 2 or Level 3 discipline referrals Number of students in high school with more than two Level 2 or Level 3 discipline referrals Number of students in middle school with discipline referrals that result in in-school and out-of school suspension, disaggregated by student subgroup Number of students in high school with discipline referrals that result in in-school and out-of-school suspension, disaggregated by student subgroup

Student Data Folders

Student data folders provide a data collection system aligned to indicators for the classroom. The folders must contain key information about indicators that teachers agree provides descriptive and supportive feedback to keep learners continually improving. They offer an organized way for students to take more responsibility for their own learning by tracking their progress around academic and other classroom expectations.

To work effectively, the collection of student data must be a systematic and systemwide process. Cross-grade and department teams must agree on systematic processes to ensure the effective use of data folders.

District Scorecard Calendar

Board Agenda	Indicator Progress Review	Administrative Council Agenda
Sept. 13	District scorecard calendar, AYP	Sept. 4
Sept. 27	Class sizes, site goals	Sept. 18
Oct. 11	Cash on hand, ADA*, % fund balance	Oct. 2
Oct. 25	Social-emotional learning survey, NWEA* growth scores, and discipline	Oct. 16
Nov. 8	State test meets or exceeds expectations	Nov. 30
Dec. 13	State test growth scores, parent satisfaction survey, and local benchmark assessments	Dec. 4
Jan. 17	Cash on hand and facility assessment	Jan. 8
Feb. 7	Excel scores and discipline reports	Jan. 29
Feb. 21	Safety, fairness, and staff satisfaction survey	Feb. 12
March 13	Scorecard overview and local benchmark assessments	March 4
April 1	Cash on hand and % fund balance	March 18
April 17	3-year budget projection and class-size report	April 8
May 8	Discipline and ISEL* assessment	April 29
May 22	Student satisfaction survey and facility assessment	May 13
June 5	Cash on hand, NWEA growth scores, graduation rate, and local benchmark assessments	May 27
Aug. 21	Scorecard overview, staff retention, and state financial rating	Aug. 5

* ADA=Average Daily [student] Attendance; NWA=Northwest Evaluation Association; ISEL=Illinois Snapshot of Early Literacy

The review of indicators is assigned to district-level administrators, who then present data, findings, analysis, and changes in action plans to school administrators. Refinements are made and results are shared with board members to allow board time and focusing on the results.

A Rubric for Achieving the Gold Standard

Indicators of Success	Confusion Around Strategic Role and Responsibilities	Understands Strategic Role and Responsibilities	The Gold Standard: Living the Strategic Role
Live your mission, vision, values, and goals	Board doesn't have an articulated, strategic vision and direction to guide work toward achieving focused organizational goals.	Board sets an articulated strategic vision and direction that result in clear, precise, and focused organizational goals by which to guide work.	Board collaboratively sets an articulated strategic vision, and direction utilizing extensive stakeholder input. This results in clear, precise, and focused organizational goals by which to guide work.
	Data alone dictate strategic priorities with little or no context provided for those data.	Goals are connected to data.	Goals and data are both aligned to strategic priorities.
	Board ignores cultural needs or expectations.	Board considers cultural needs in determining strategic priorities.	Strategic priorities account for cultural needs.
		Some board energy is focused on strategic priorities, but most of the board's energy is spent elsewhere.	Most of the board's energy is spent on strategic priorities.
Build a collaborative culture through shared leadership.	Board reacts to and focuses upon individual acts of improvement that are not aligned with other district initiatives or desired outcomes.	Board has a commitment to continuous improvement of the school district.	Board creates and sustains a culture of ongoing change and continuous improvement.

continued on next page →

Indicators of Success	Confusion Around Strategic Role and Responsibilities	Understands Strategic Role and Responsibilities	The Gold Standard: Living the Strategic Role
Build a collaborative culture through shared leadership.	Board's existing structures and processes are unclear and inconsistently deployed.	Board uses structures and processes to keep it strategically focused.	Board structures and processes are systematic and deployed through all levels of the school district.
	Board-superintendent relationship isn't secure because a lack of trust by each side in the other doesn't allow for unity of purpose.	Board recognizes that a strong partnership with the superintendent is essential to organizational success, but doesn't consistently act as a partner in making decisions.	Board-superintendent partnership reflects a high degree of trust and collaboration, which allows the district to fulfill its vision and mission.
	The lack of collaboration and trust among the strategic, tactical, and operational roles results in independent silos of unaligned efforts.	Board recognizes that collaboration and mutual trust are necessary to form a sustained partnership among the three roles, but doesn't consistently make decisions based upon this recognition.	Board consistently expects and promotes collaboration and mutual trust across the three roles.
	Board infrequently utilizes input groups; when it does, it usually doesn't follow the group's recommendations.	Board utilizes staff and community input groups to help set its strategic priorities, but might not fulfill their expectations of future shared decision-making.	Board charges to staff and community input groups account for engagement of those groups in future collaborative and role-appropriate decision-making.
	Board doesn't assume the responsibility of being visionary because of the community's desire for stability, or it ignores the desire of stability in order to promote rapid changes.	Board recognizes that its responsibility for visionary change may conflict with the community's desire for ongoing stability.	Board effectively and collaboratively balances organizational stability with visionary change.

continued on next page →

Indicators of Success	Confusion Around Strategic Role and Responsibilities	Understands Strategic Role and Responsibilities	The Gold Standard: Living the Strategic Role
Have data drive decision-making.	Board has insufficient data to guide its strategic priorities.	Board systematically uses data to focus on its strategic priorities, but the data determined for collection are defined mainly by the board. Board utilizes a scorecard to identify and track key strategic priority indicators and report progress to the community but occasionally acts independently from its scorecard data.	Board systematically uses data from learners, classrooms, and schools to focus upon its strategic priorities.
	Board has no district performance scorecard to identify and track progress toward achieving strategic priorities, or has a scorecard and uses it to micromanage.	Board uses data to assess both processes and outcomes.	Board utilizes a scorecard to identify and monitor key strategic priority indicators and reports progress to the community. It consistently bases its actions on its analysis of scorecard data.
	Board is process-driven rather than outcomes-driven. Processes are random and inconsistent.	Board decisions are impersonal, objective, and professional.	Board continually ensures that organizational processes yield outcome measurements.
	Board decisions are personal and subjective.	Board recognizes the need for research to inform decision-making and takes on the task of researching desired standards of rigor.	Board decisions reflect a selfless visionary perspective.

continued on next page ↓

Indicators of Success	Confusion Around Strategic Role and Responsibilities	Understands Strategic Role and Responsibilities	The Gold Standard: Living the Strategic Role
Have data drive decision-making.	Board either performs its own research independent of staff or fails to establish rigorous standards for research.		Board sets rigorous standards for research but allows staff to perform or arrange for research.
Align board responsibilities and behaviors with school district goals and actions.	Board has difficulty consistently staying within a strategic role.	Board willingly embraces a strategic role.	Board actively promotes and follows a collaborative, formal decision-making cycle.
	Board meddles in other role responsibilities by not staying within the limits of the strategic role.	Board understands and adheres to the limits of the strategic role with occasional reminders to do so from administration.	Board members consistently self-monitor in adhering to the limits of the strategic role.
	Board ignores role expertise at other levels of the system.	Board recognizes that there are different levels of role expertise within the system.	Board actively encourages collaborative efforts that tap into levels of expertise found at each role.
	Board doesn't collaboratively set realistic timeframes, thereby imposing its timeframes on tacticians and operationalists.	Board sets timelines for district goals that realistically account for the needs of administrators and teachers.	Board solicits realistic strategic, tactical, and operational timeframes as part of its strategic planning and recognizes that timeframes need to be set collaboratively.

continued on next page →

Indicators of Success	Confusion Around Strategic Role and Responsibilities	Understands Strategic Role and Responsibilities	The Gold Standard: Living the Strategic Role
Align board responsibilities and behaviors with school district goals and actions.	Board members take partisan positions rather than addressing the merits of issues, or don't support split-vote decisions based on the merits of the issues.	Board members vote individually based upon the merits of the issues and agree to support split-vote decisions.	Board members reach consensus upon the merits of issues prior to voting.
Build system accountability at all levels.	Board has insufficient data to be accountable to the community for organizational progress.	Board has the data it needs to be accountable to the community for organizational progress but doesn't consistently share them.	Board uses appropriate data for strategic decision-making and is accountable to the community for continuous improvement.
	Board either doesn't have the appropriate data for the goal it's assessing or doesn't know how to properly analyze the appropriate data to guide continuous improvement.	Board has the right data to make strategic decisions.	Board knows how to analyze the right data to guide continuous improvement.
	Board evaluates staff members subjectively, absent utilizing objective and rigorous standards for performance.	Board knows the difference between monitoring and evaluating organizational performance.	Board monitors organizational performance while allowing evaluation of individual performance to occur at the tactical and operational levels.

continued on next page ↓

The School Board Fieldbook © 2009 Solution Tree Press • www.solution-tree.com
Visit **go.solution-tree.com/schoolboards** to download this page.

Indicators of Success	Confusion Around Strategic Role and Responsibilities	Understands Strategic Role and Responsibilities	The Gold Standard: Living the Strategic Role
Build system accountability at all levels.	Board confuses the evaluation of individual performance with the monitoring of organizational performance.	Board sets the standards of rigor for evaluation of performance, but still monitors evaluation processes.	Board sets the standards of rigor for evaluating staff performance, which is done by tacticians and operationalists.
	Board micromanages by establishing action plans that drive strategic priorities represented in the scorecard.	Board doesn't link scorecard priorities and action plans.	Board allows tacticians to determine the plans required to reach the strategic goals represented in the scorecard.
	Board hasn't established a relationship between its budget and strategic priorities.	Board directs fiscal resources toward strategic priorities.	Board budget is based upon its strategic priorities.
Communicate at all levels.	Board doesn't distinguish between strategic, tactical, and operational data and micromanages as a result.	Board understands that some data it receives aren't essential to its strategic decision-making role; rather, existing data inform the board of data that other stakeholders need.	Board consistently distinguishes between data needed for strategic decision-making and data needed for tactical and operational decision-making.
	Board's scorecard backup data either insufficiently explain scorecard metrics used or are too detailed for reporting.	Board's scorecard backup data accurately explain scorecard metrics but are too detailed because they have gone beyond the scorecard's purpose.	Board's scorecard backup data accurately explain scorecard metrics without utilizing data that are more appropriate for the tactical and operational levels.

continued on next page ↓

Indicators of Success	Confusion Around Strategic Role and Responsibilities	Understands Strategic Role and Responsibilities	The Gold Standard: Living the Strategic Role
Communicate at all levels.	Board lacks bridge structures with community, administration, and union groups and fails to communicate effectively.	Board understands that bridge structures are required to effectively communicate with community, administration, and union audiences.	Board utilizes communication bridges to community, administration, and union groups, and refrains from establishing such bridges to operational staff.
	Board members don't follow the complaint process and address complaints inappropriate to their strategic role.	Board has a formalized complaint process and follows it, but still wants to determine outcomes when it doesn't agree with the outcomes the complaint process and board policies describe.	Board doesn't leave its strategic role in following its formal complaint process.
	Board doesn't articulate clear, challenging, and rigorous targets, nor does it acknowledge or celebrate success at all levels of the organization.	Board takes responsibility for articulating challenge and rigor expected of the organization and for celebrating success at all levels of the system that improves organizational performance, but doesn't always make this a priority.	Board consistently and effectively promotes challenging and rigorous goals for the school district, while recognizing and celebrating success at all levels.
	Board doesn't recognize that different roles and audiences require different communication strategies.	Board members recognize that communicating with other roles and audiences is more difficult than communicating with each other.	Board uses a variety of strategies to appropriately communicate with different roles and stakeholders while remaining within its strategic role.

continued on next page →

The School Board Fieldbook © 2009 Solution Tree Press • www.solution-tree.com
Visit **go.solution-tree.com/schoolboards** to download this page.

Indicators of Success	Confusion Around Strategic Role and Responsibilities	Understands Strategic Role and Responsibilities	The Gold Standard: Living the Strategic Role
Communicate at all levels.	Board either doesn't respond to an individual's needs within a reasonable time or responds too quickly, without confirming whether that need is validated by objective data.	Board responds to an individual's needs within a reasonable timeframe.	Board understands that responding to an individual's needs requires a balance between taking time to validate those needs and responding in a timely fashion.
	Board isn't aware that its use of a scorecard might be threatening to some groups or is aware and still uses the scorecard without accounting for or being concerned with the threat or its impact on the group.	Board understands a scorecard's message can be appropriate for the community and at the same time be threatening to staff.	Board ensures that staff isn't threatened by board's use of a scorecard to report progress to the community.
	Board seldom, if ever, addresses its strategic priorities by placing the scorecard on its public meeting agenda or discussing those priorities in any other public way.	Board regularly uses its scorecard to publicly focus upon its strategic priorities.	Board uses a scorecard at each public meeting to focus upon its strategic priorities and measurable results.
	Board is so busy listening to the public that it fails to complete its business, or spends insufficient time listening to the public before completing its business.	Board understands that its need to conduct its business might occasionally be in conflict with the public's need to interface with the board.	Board balances its need to conduct its business with the public's need to be heard.

continued on next page →

Indicators of Success	Confusion Around Strategic Role and Responsibilities	Understands Strategic Role and Responsibilities	The Gold Standard: Living the Strategic Role
Communicate at all levels.	Board doesn't understand how its decision-making process affects the public's acceptance of board decisions.	Board understands that its decision-making process, as publicly modeled, will affect whether the public accepts the decisions it makes.	Board understands that its public modeling of an effective decision-making process is as important as any of the decisions it makes.
Focus on stake-holder (parent, student, teacher, community) satisfaction.	Board isn't concerned with stakeholder opinions or needs as it makes decisions.	Board cares about stakeholder opinions but only intermittently utilizes perception surveys as an objective way to identify those opinions.	Board uses a specific schedule for the collection and analysis of perception survey data.
	Board doesn't collect stakeholder perception data, fails to use what it collects, or uses them in isolation, thereby making inappropriate assumptions and decisions.	Board uses perception surveys to identify stakeholder desires.	Board regularly combines perception data with other indicators of success to determine long-term and short-term district priorities.
	Board acts in isolation based upon an individual's need without first validating that need.	Board understands it shouldn't act upon an individual's need alone but doesn't always have objective data to rely upon in determining the validity of that individual's need.	Board links an individual's need with more objective data to determine its validity.

The School Board Fieldbook © 2009 Solution Tree Press • www.solution-tree.com
Visit **go.solution-tree.com/schoolboards** to download this page.

References and Resources

Barr, R., & Parrett, W. (2007). *The kids left behind: Catching up the underachieving children of poverty.* Bloomington, IN: Solution Tree Press.

Benjamin, S. (2007). *The quality rubric: A systematic approach for implementing quality principles and tools in classrooms and schools.* Milwaukee, WI: American Society for Quality Press.

Bernhardt, V. (2002). *Using data to improve student learning: Middle schools.* Larchmont, NY: Eye on Education.

Bossidy, L., & Charan, R. (2002). *Execution: The discipline of getting things done.* New York: Crown Business.

Buckingham, M., & Coffman, C. (1999). *First break all the rules: What the world's greatest managers do differently.* New York: Simon & Schuster.

Canfield, J. M., Hansen, M. V., & Hewitt, L. (2000). *The power of focus: How to hit your business, personal and financial targets with absolute certainty.* Deerfield Beach, FL: Health Communications.

Carter, L. (2007). *Total instructional alignment: From standards to student success.* Bloomington, IN: Solution Tree Press.

Center for Association Leadership. (2006). *7 measures of success: What remarkable associations do that others don't.* Washington, DC: American Society of Association Executives and the Center for Association Leadership.

Chappuis, S., Stiggins, R., Arter, J., & Chappuis, J. (2005). *Assessment FOR learning: An action guide for school leaders.* Portland, OR: Assessment Training Institute.

Collins, J. (2001). *Good to great: Why some companies make the leap . . . and others don't.* New York: Harper Business.

Covey, S. (1990). *Principle-centered leadership.* New York: Simon & Schuster.

Covey, S. (1994). *First things first.* New York: Simon & Schuster.

Dobyns, L., & Crawford-Mason, C. (1994). *Thinking about quality: Progress, wisdom, and the Deming philosophy.* Boston and New York: Houghton-Mifflin Company.

Dolan, W. P. (1994). *Restructuring our schools: A primer on systemic change.* Kansas City, MO: Systems and Organizations.

DuFour, R., DuFour, R., Eaker, R., & Karhanek, G. (2004). *Whatever it takes: How professional learning communities respond when kids don't learn.* Bloomington, IN: Solution Tree Press (formerly National Educational Service).

DuFour, R., DuFour, R., Eaker, R., & Many, T. (2006). *Learning by doing: A handbook for professional learning communities at work.* Bloomington, IN: Solution Tree Press.

DuFour, R., Eaker, R., & DuFour, R. (Eds.). (2005). *On common ground: The power of professional learning communities.* Bloomington, IN: Solution Tree Press (formerly National Educational Service).

Fullan, M. (2001). *Leading in a culture of change.* San Francisco: Jossey-Bass.

Fullan, M. (2006). *Turnaround leadership.* San Francisco: Jossey-Bass.

Fullan, M. (2008). *Six secrets of change.* San Francisco: Jossey-Bass.

Fullan, M., Hill, P., & Crevola, C. (2007). *Breakthrough.* San Francisco: Jossey-Bass.

Holcomb, E. L. (2004). *Getting excited about data: Combining people, passion, and proof to maximize student achievement* (2nd ed.). Thousand Oaks, CA: Corwin.

Jenkins, L. (1997). *Improving student learning: Applying Deming's quality principles to classrooms.* Milwaukee, WI: American Society for Quality Press.

Jim Shipley and Associates. (2002). *Teacher and student partnerships: Part I and Part II* (2nd ed.). North Redington Beach, FL: Author.

Jim Shipley and Associates. (2006). *Continuous classroom improvement: A systems approach to improving learning results.* North Redington Beach, FL: Author.

Jim Shipley and Associates. (2007). *Classroom performance excellence: Focus on refinement and improvement.* North Redington Beach, FL: Author.

Lezotte, L., & McKee, K. (2006). *Stepping up: Leading the charge to improve our schools.* Okemos, MI: Effective Schools Products, Ltd.

Marzano, R. (2007). *The art and science of teaching: A comprehensive framework for effective instruction.* Alexandria, VA: Association for Supervision and Curriculum Development.

O'Neill, J., & Conzemius, A. (2002). *The handbook for SMART school teams.* Bloomington, IN: Solution Tree Press (formerly National Educational Service).

O'Neill, J., & Conzemius, A. (2006). *The power of SMART goals: Using goals to improve student learning.* Bloomington, IN: Solution Tree Press.

Reeves, D. (2006). *The learning leader: How to focus school improvement for better results.* Alexandria, VA: Association for Supervision and Curriculum Development.

Reeves, D. (Ed.). (2007). *Ahead of the curve: The power of assessment to transform teaching and learning.* Bloomington, IN: Solution Tree Press.

Rosenthal, J., & Masarech, M. A. (2003). High performance cultures: How values can drive business results. *Journal of Organizational Excellence, 22*(2), 3–18.

Schmoker, M. (1999). *Results: The key to continuous school improvement* (2nd ed.). Alexandria, VA: Association for Supervision and Curriculum Development.

Schmoker, M. (2006). *Results now: How we can achieve unprecedented improvement in teaching and learning.* Alexandria, VA: Association for Supervision and Curriculum Development.

Senge, P. (1990). *The fifth discipline.* New York: Doubleday.

Senge, P., Schein, E., du Geus, A., & Gallwey, T. (1998). *The new workplace: Transforming the character and the culture of our organizations.* Waltham, MA: Pegasus Communications, Inc.

Stiggins, R. (2006, November-December). Assessment FOR learning: A key to motivation and achievement. *Phi Delta Kappan EDge, 2*(2), 1–20.

Studer, Q. (2003). *Hardwiring for excellence.* Gulf Breeze, FL: Firestarter Publishing.

Studer, Q. (2008). *Results that last.* Hoboken, NJ: John Wiley and Sons.

Wahlstrom, D. (2002). *Using data to improve student achievement.* Suffolk, VA: Successline.

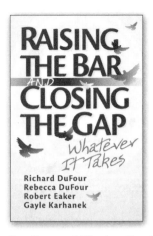
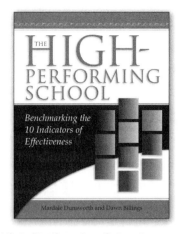
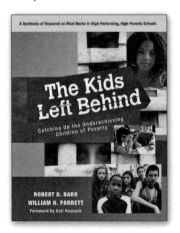
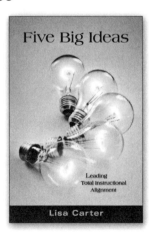

Solution Tree

Solution Tree's mission is to advance the work of our authors. By working with the best researchers and educators worldwide, we strive to be the premier provider of innovative publishing, in-demand events, and inspired professional development designed to transform education to ensure that all students learn.

AMERICAN ASSOCIATION OF SCHOOL ADMINISTRATORS

The American Association of School Administrators, founded in 1865, is the professional organization for more than 13,000 educational leaders across the United States. AASA's mission is to support and develop effective school system leaders who are dedicated to the highest quality public education for all children.